POISON: IN MAGIC LAND

First printing.

Softcover: ISBN 978-0-9644304-9-5
Vanderblümen Publications
P.O. Box 626
La Mesa, CA 91944

Printed in the United States of America

Vanderblümen Publications
La Mesa, California

If there has been anything that I have learned in my 17 years of life, it would be:

"One may never know what it truly feels like to stand up, if one has never fallen down before."

I was inspired to write this book during the hardest years of my life. From age fifteen to seventeen, I had walked on this Earth confused and worried about who I truly was, asking myself, "Am I normal?" trying to check myself into a reality. I spent many days contemplating on each of the steps I was taking. I always searched for the answers to life in books, and if not just books, I'd search through people. My mother once told me, as she complimented me, "You have the desire to want to know things. You sit down, search and analyze concepts and ideas, until in your own way, you figure them out. That's what makes you special."

I want to thank my mother for raising me the way that she did. No matter her low points in life, she always taught to me, to respect and love my neighbors. As a young kid, I was exposed to a life that could've taken me down either two roads. One, a road of pain and destruction. The other, filled with peace and construction. Construction of self. It took me many years to grasp onto the idea of who I really am without my mother's eyes on me.

Even today, I ask God to reveal that answer to me. Each day, my goal is to take one step further in my journey that reveals to me who I want to be and who God wants me to be. Had it not been for the love of God, I would not have the determination that I have to get where I am aiming for in life. Thank you Lord for all of your blessings. I am grateful for each and every one of them. For you are forever in my eyes and worthy to be praised.

Last but not least, I would like to share what I've learned through watching people from primary school through high school. Having the "brightest life" can mean that in the darkness, you are the darkest. And sometimes, the ones who shy away from the light and live in the dark, are the people who usually shine the brightest once they gain the courage to speak. Sometimes, I don't know which one I am. Sometimes, it kills me to not know, and sometimes, it doesn't matter, not one bit.

However, when it does matter, I'm searching to find myself by looking at life through many different lenses. I had to step out of my comfort zone in order to write a book about love. It wasn't easy at all. Surrounding myself with the influences of my generation, whether positive or negative, made my task just a bit less stressful. For everyone that has known me, chatted with me, gave me a hug on a rough day, asked me how I was doing, or just simply smiled at me, I would like to thank you. For you may have been one of my biggest inspirations when I chose to write these stories.

To my family, friends, and lovers all around the world. Thank you for supporting me and being such a loving foundation. For it is when I see you all, holding my books, reading my words, and deeply being touched, what truly puts a smile on my face. I thank the ambitious reader that is reading this right now. You do not know how much happiness you are simply sending my way. I cannot say thank you enough. Love.

#ForTheLovers

Hey, sometimes you're going to have to learn it all by yourself.
You're going to hit a couple of bumps in the road, so what.
Fellas, yeah she's going to make a couple of tears fall, so what.
Ladies, trust me, oh he's going to mess up a few times, but so what.

Mothers, yes, teens will be teens.
Fathers, if she loves the boy, she loves the boy.
I know you think you know it all, parents.
I know you've been there and done that before,
But guess what?

You got it, "so what"
Everyone learns different. Not one of us have the *same* love story.
Sometimes, it starts off shaky, like a rocket launching into space.
And other times, it may start off smooth, like a kick-push on marble floors.
All that I'm trying to say is,
Stop trying to learn about love from the eyes of everyone else (just for a second)
Learn it from the experiences behind your own two eyes.
The ride is better when you're driving your own mind,
Not someone else's.

There are millions of answers to the question,
What is love?

I just hope, you can build the desire, to one day finally, find your own.

POISON: **IN MAGIC** LAND

"I feel like, everyone loves you. Duh. Because you're you. But I love you on an unexplainable and no comprehending level. I love the real you, the depressed 2 AM pessimist Terrance; just as much as I love the 2 in the afternoon optimist Terrance."

"I mean, life goes on, and everyone loves you. Including Terrance. So if things don't work out. Terrance will still love Terrance. Even I, will still love Terrance. Everyone that knows him, will love him. You never lose."

"Everyone means nothing, if I don't have you."

"The more we know, the more we realize we don't know. So we fiend for knowledge. I love that."

"Why is it that we feel annoyed by a person that gives us love and affection every day when really, that's all we want?"

"Just like everything in life, things come and go. Some things are forever mentally, and some aren't. I guess it's just all in our mind. Once we don't want something, it's hard for us to even understand why we wanted it in the first place. Maybe we only lose track of what we truly want, because we find something else that we want. And that is, our replacement, our alternative, hope, and new solution, momentarily. Until we want something else."

"Gosh. I love you..."

"You're always telling me how great I am. And I get it, I mean, I do. Thank you. But it's time that you start to notice and tell yourself how great you are. Tell me, what is it that you really want from me in life?"

"For you to be happy and successful in whatever you want to do."

"And if I can't?"

"Then, I can't."

FOR THE LOVERS

Table of Contents

POISON: In Magic Land

Introduction: Dark Spruced Forest

INTRODUCTION

Back when I was a young boy, I never understood what love really was. In fact, till this day, I won't dare make any promises that I can clearly explain to a soul exactly what it is. Somewhere down the line between the soak and wet age of 15 and the rough sprouting age of 17, I figured it wouldn't hurt if I wrote stories about such a universal idea.

At first, I was into writing cute love poems. You know, the type of poems descriptively written for an imaginary lover as a child. You know, something very cliché. Something very, what's it called, oh yeah, I got it, "unoriginal." Something in the same nature of that crappy ole' junk, "Dear so and so, here's a poem for you that I wrote. I was up all night thinking of your beautiful smile..."

After I reached a certain level of maturity, writing poems such as grew to fade away from my interest. I grew a drive to dig deeper when I would write my stories. Forget about scratching the surface, my objective was finding out why. Why do I love? Why do we love? What makes me want to love? Is love just a fantasy? Or am I, in some cases believing in what everyone else believes in?

When was the last time you've heard a happy human say, "Love isn't real." Keep in mind that I do say, a "happy" human. It's backwards, in our generation to think such a thought. If we are to ever hear those words, that person (whomever the speaker is) deserves a slap to the face.

Why? Well, don't you think it's quite odd that someone would say "love isn't real" when there are millions of examples of love being spread and given to you right now? Why is one so brave to say that love is not real? Or that love does not exist?

Let's be honest here, I am no master on love. I am no therapist, nor any kind of counselor who has all of the right answers about who needs to love who, or who doesn't need to be loving what. I'm just here to tell my stories about what I've experienced in my 17 years of life and conclude that love is real. My job is to tell the story from the eye of one who has been a sneaky witness to everything surrounding all concepts of love. My job is to withdraw from personal opinions of what this idea of love truly is, and provide true stories that can be viewed as lessons of love. My job is also to provide to you, feelings, thoughts, and questions, which will reveal some secrets from the world of the youth.

You may feel as if you know what love is already. And you also may feel that you cannot learn anything about love. But just like everyone else who is determined and mentally ready to find love, you can find it too.

Here's the treat, your eyes are my paper, these lines are the paint, and I am the artist painting the picture. Or should I say, illustrating the map. There is no location to Magic Land, there are no maps, highways, or back-way alleys. There is nothing, but God, the devil, and I, helpless to find the difference between my fantasies and reality. If clarity is only a state of mind, then there should be no problems.

*However, as teenagers, it is quite difficult to scope the differences between **lust and love (fantasies and reality)** Who is to say which is which? And who can teach what the principles of true love is to a teenager better than a teenager? One who has been eager to "love" since sandbox days. It's actually quite a lesson to learn wouldn't chu say? There is no progress without failure. I've heard that plenty of times, and after falling on my knees a couple of times, I finally learned how it feels to stand strong. I can now see the differences between fantasy and reality. No, I am no professional. You can learn a lot from a dummy who's bound to learn a lot. In fact, that's another lesson in itself, isn't it?*

"Ha, a 17-year-old with enough guts to try and teach a little something about love. What in the world does he know about love?"

The mighty L-O-V-E. Well, like Mama always used to say, "Boy, it's not always what you know, it's who you know."

These short chapters derived from the close influences I surrounded myself with throughout my teenage years. Whether it be friends, family, associates, movies, conversations with strangers, you name it. This is where it all began. The next chapter contains a collage of poems about the many different concepts of love, from a young man's perspective – as he views the experience of love through a female's life.

For every two, indulged in thoughts and actions, driven by love. This is for you all. This is for the lovers. From me to you. Based on true experiences.

Dark Spruced Forest

She picked her head up from a pile of soft leaves matted together forming a fluffy pillow. All night long she had danced with autumn leaves drizzling down on her enigma. It was dark and misty blue. She pushed away from the moist soil she had been resting in. Onto her feet, she stood to stop and stare at the beauty in her presence. It felt as if she were still dreaming. In both physical and mental states, she began to travel. Ahead of her was a narrow path. Close up she could see everything.

As life was distant from her eyesight, nature appeared to be sought in blurs. She wasn't blind to the snakes slithering in a slow motion near the thorns in the garden to the left of her. The branches on the trees on both sides of this narrow path whispered a chilly melody. A soft echo from the winds' voice trapped her inside of her own stage of understanding. She understood her fears but held onto her courage to block her nearest thoughts of giving up. She had a goal. A goal worth achieving so much that she would do just about anything to get it accomplished.

She remembered having a conversation and receiving a gift from a man who was meditating next to a stack of newspapers and a box of peaches and grapevines. He was old and looked like he had been living on the land for many years. He stopped in the middle of meditation and the two made eye contact. She said a silent prayer, and took a step towards him trying to scurry past. He grabbed a waist bag, stood up, and gave it to her. He saw the dull look in her eyes and she saw the passion in his. With his eyes locked firmly onto her soul, he told her, "Go! Go find it!" and she went on searching. Just like that.

As she searched the land, she was blessed with many gifts. Rather than accepting these gifts, she decided to go on and focus on finding love. (The love that was taught to her by the world) When love was right in her face she let it go. She was distracted and manipulated by the fruits of nature. In all of her time in this forest, the winds whispered, "What are you looking for?" and in her head she knew the answer. She was looking for him. She was looking for me. She was looking for love.

Her name, is Sasha. Sasha has a past just like everyone else living. She uses her past to motivate her towards taking the right steps into her future. Sasha wanted so many more people to know her story. Nobody knew what really happened to her. Not even me at one point. She wanted someone to show her what it felt like to be vulnerable and affectionate.

She struggled to understand that it is common for mankind to hide their affectionate side. Not everyone enjoys being vulnerable. She thought that it would be simple to find love. Simple? Yes, simple. And we all know, there's nothing simple about love when one is experiencing its highs and lows. She found that out the hard way. Nothing in this life comes easy. And before she could fully grasp that, this is what she had to go through. She reached down into the waist bag and pulled out a tiny notebook. In this notebook, is where she jotted down her thoughts, emotions and obstacles while searching to find love. These, are her stories...

Sasha is rather than a true character in the story, but "SHE" is a living metaphor. Sasha represents the female side of love. Throughout the story she is used to embody and present the perspective of a young woman who is searching to find love.

For the Lovers

Isn't this, what they've been waiting for?
The cutting of a ruby red ribbon
The grand opening to the center
Kissing the midpoints of disappointment
Isn't this, what they wanted?

From the minor minds,
Searching to find, a four letter word
Covered in dirt, soothing what hurts
If we could measure,
And only if we could
Would it matter if it never existed?
So optimistic and willingly
Still, we all search to find.

Unfortunately, this idea, found through similar ways,
Through identical phases, on a million faces,
Between a million minds,
Power created that lonely rose that grew from the pavement
Love...

In the bedroom, or the kitchen
On carpets in the basements
From writing it away,
To working with erasers
To numb the pain the vacant created.
Clarity is a station
A state of mind
Can I take you?

On a trip
Buckle up; don't you slip on the liquid
Drop, or drip, on the carpet
In the darkest section of our hearts
Let's find it?

In our minds, close the blinds
Keep your eyes, open
I said, keep your eyes open
Here's the key,
I said it, so here is the key
Welcome,
Make yourself at home
And when you feel alone...

Close your blinds, finally.
From ventricle cuts to physical lust
Isn't this what
They've been waiting for?

Sasha's Dream

Growing up on the right side of the Coronado Bridge,
Bound to corners surrounding Imperial,
I ate the cereal,
Lucky Charms every morning right around the time
The sun started to shine and light my split-image.

We grew up a couple blocks away from danger,
She never fell victim to the eyes of any stranger,
Or poe men strung over low ends,
They seemed to hang her, on carriages where their minds rest,
She skipped through pitiful dialect,
Such an intellectual female – she was fond with the detailed
Dialogue heard from the sidewalks, distant.
Knuckleheads would take her to the smoke shop to get lifted,
Hoping that all her problems like wishes, would drift.

My mama was on the water.
And father, a window shopper,
Former ex-convict, playa, drug dealer, and panty dropper,
Used to interrupt my dreams - fingers in my cookie jar.
I scream "stop" but his knuckles did not,
Silently slide violent kisses on my back,
My nose, more red, than my roses,
My violet patches engraved, took control,
Over – abusive.

Caressed as a kid and he never felt guilty of it.
No rubbers just under covers, he told me to keep it tucked,
In my pillow sheets, I sunk those lovely dreams into misery.

"Sasha, I don't mean to bother. Just come a little closer. This won't be long. Appreciate the moments that I'm sober. You're so beautiful baby. Now listen, to your father. No problems tonight, alright? Okay baby, now bend over."

Blindfolded, he stole her virginity as a saint,
St. Mary on her dresser; she was catholic.
But called on Jesus when she felt attacked.

As friends, we walked hand in hand,
In Magic Land, we'd feed comfort,
As lovers – as two true undiscovered-souls.

She had slim model legs and a cocoa brown face.
Coca-Cola bottles - matched her body frame.
On occasions, we set foot in a set, to hear "what set you claim?"
"Is this your man, you're looking like a dime, can I get your name?"
compliments.

I'd say "Yes, I'm with him." to boost his confidence,
Locked arms together,
My drive - tested his conscience-when
I whispered,
"I dare you to let go and lose this vital grip."

"Terrance, I need you"

Now, my heart racing my footsteps balancing worries,
We head out in a hurry in a rush, to run and feel secure.
Her eyes speak to the thoughts I store,
Her body language screaming out "Baby, it's yours."

Her blood drips, and I fall to my knees, just to pray for her.
911's a call away, but I can't tell he's raping her.
Cause if I tell, may her soul dwell in a coffin.
**At least that's what she said when I picked up the phone to call
them.**
She begged me to stay silent. It killed me like a virus,
To know that she's embarrassed to speak on the pain and violence.

We hugged on 47th street, and I told him I'll be fine,
Came back the next day with long cuts under my eye,
Marks around my neck,
Back at home - I opened wide - and had a taste of death.
Love kisses never existed.

Bitter dreams of our past - shaped our future,
Illusions came with a crash,

Hearts formed sweet and sticky tears,
Everlasting pain is what we sat on in the grass
Before the sun kissed the ocean
We promised to come back.

Farewell, tip the hat,
Close the cap, sip the glass,
Take it off, just relax...

Blood dripped from the center,
Where's the match?
He burned her soul,
Manipulating the mind over masses
Mind on the mistress, he did get distracted
As for Sasha,
She was still dreaming.
Where was I?

Peek-A-Boo

Geez, I never came back.
I was only 12,
I didn't know that you would really need me.
We were 12.
I guess I modeled superheroes freely,
But I had no superpowers in those hours,
You were screaming.

When he covered your eyes,
Did you see my face?
Peek-a-boo I didn't see you.
I feel ashamed.
I didn't know that happened every single day,
I believed you,
When you smiled and said "Yeah, I'm okay."

I should've rescued you,
Instead, I let it happen,
At 12, you were miserable.
And I was just a kid.

We shared pain,
But I didn't feel it like you did.

You cried and tears did nothing at all,
You said you saw with droopy eyes,
That man's downfall,
And all I see,
Is everything that I didn't do,
How today - do I still feel love from you?
How could you – love - me?

If I never came,
Back, how do you feel the same?
How do you think of me-
When you stare from that window pane?
You don't feel the pain,
But oh, I feel it.

Forgive me,
And drown me in your loving nutrition.

Can I give you a new feeling – after the fact?
I apologize for the nights I never came back

But I'm here now.

Nutrishin

What,
Does it mean?
To dream about someone?

To dream about someone,
You think, is real.
Can we call those people unreal?
They heal us while we need healing,
Are they human, like us?

What,
Is that feeling?

What,
Does it mean when one,
Becomes too addicted to such a substance
What happens when they love it?
A little too much,
What happens when too much equals crazy?
What,
Does it mean, when the same equals a maybe?
And maybe - equals a heart,
That creeps in hibernation
Sleeps through hunt seasons
Finding reasons its role is aching.
Lying to be okay,
When it hurts, it's all creative.

You create the gold vase,
Cremate the pain laying,
In piles,

What,
Does it mean?
To dream about someone?

When that someone doesn't exist.

Only in your mind,
Only in one state,
One stage of sleep,
How do you know?
When you wake from every dream,
What's a dream, and what isn't?

A lonely lifetime is the *distance*.
But living here, you-   will never **know**
the *difference*.

Differences

And as for myself,
I watched her.
Resting with her right foot over her left
Hair slicked back to the left
Left her emotions
Before a wink with her left eye
She began to write her pain

Right about when her lover passed her mind
I made the right decision
As she, passed my eyes
Intercepting intentions, she wept.

On her shoulder, there they were, she kept,
It all imprinted like a lion had carved into her skin,
The darkest words, "I've been misused"
I was right, but left the clues
I missed my cues
On a quest to find the comforting questions
I missed,
Those, I suppose, I failed the assessment.

Her eyes screwed, proving she was a blessing for worse.
Nothing less than a blessing, bless the mess of her curves.
She looked through me,
Inside, she cried, "Who are you?"

"Who am I?
Don't you know? I'm right where I desire.
I would, stay this close forever, but you know forever dies
The wheels around your eyelids
Remind me of the times
We would dig to find a finer set of fire
Foolish minds
Impatient
Fueling what was left behind

"Do you mind? I am peace"

Now, left foot over her right. Hair held tight in a messy bun
Mind on a million bright thoughts based on love…
Piped down in night gowns
Left emotion beside her
Insider her, rested I
Riding all her pain away, she writes it all away
She hides; but it's okay.
So do you, right?

Right,
Lost within the lows of loves high
The difference,
Is just about every right - builds suspension
But we've missed our cues
Love struck ducking intermission

Too focused on the mission
We stood at the buildings,
Building, fighting all of our feelings
Fighting this ride,
When really we were just riding along.

We would hide in the rhythm,
To find ourselves in the song,
And we would groove,
Until Luther started taking control,
Yes, we bumped with the bass,
Until the bass kissed our souls,
And finally as it started to decrease in its tone,
We moved confused
Alone and together,
Together alone.

Now my right foot, crossed on my lap
Without a sad song playing,
Totally wrapped,
Baby, what am I saying?
Have this feeling over and over
Until it brings closure,
Without exposure,

The only reason left,
Is getting closer.
Besides dreaming, without nourishment and no teaching,
We can do it together,
Until the sun stops beaming.

So, let's get closer,
And find it all together,
Our answers are limited,
But our questions are forever.
Right?

When I Met Her

Coming to California,
Foreigner, unto fortune.
Fantasizing for fantasy,
Dashing to find importance,
Is this love?
Or just another stimulated buzz?

I can't really tell you how it feels.
She burns and I yearn,
For all of her attention,
My eyes wanted to listen.
But my ears didn't hear,
Vibe ratings.

Pretty young thing?
Or a fine little lady?
She was more like a beauty queen,
Michael?

"Remember to always think twice"

It was dark, and vibrant.
It was loud, and silent.
It was vague,
As she dampened me in her sweet confinement.

It was ugly, and beautiful.
It was nothing but truth.
So I reached into her back pocket,
Depositing proof.

Poof, be gone.
She was very confused,
And spun around in circles,
Disliking the vibe from a loop,
Oops, we moved too fast,
And came up too – short,

Waving the new news
Into her ear just to sooth,

Smooth criminal tendencies,
Remember to think twice.

All along the way,
I tried preventing her mind,
To steal the truths about me,
It wasn't easy to find – a love - like this.

Ooh Boy!

Ooh boy, I love you so…
One day I will let you know,
Until then, keep those eyes on blue…

Ooh boy, hold me close,
You don't have to let them know,
That I, keep these eyes on you…

Make me feel worthless,
A million pictures,
Sitting in my furnace,
Baby, I'll burn them.
Baby, I'll burn them.
Never mind it, only if you come from hind' the curtains.
I'm burning.

For you love,
Ooh boy, I love you so…
And you keep me on my 10 toes,
Sadly, happiness is what I'm only asking for,
Four out of five times,
You tell me one lie,
Line up the vibes that combine in the dark night,
I want to leave,
This I heard in the grapevine

I want to sing,
But you burned all my tapes.
High cracked vinyls,
You hide those to create,
Mood swings between you and we,
I don't like that,
I need, you.
Can you, please not fight back?

Ooh boy, I love you so.
I don't think you're wise enough to truly know
All - the - love - I store - for you

Sincerely,

Sasha...

Just a Friend

Remember those days,
When he or she was just a friend?
Just a smile, for a little while
Until a smile was just a grin,
Just a moment,
Just a minute,
"It's just tension"
"We're pretending"

Watch those dimples
It's the simple,
Things in life that always stick.
Isn't it?
Is that person just a friend?
Again repeating what we've been,
Through already,
Are you ready?
Will you ride until the end?

From a smile, there came a grin
From the lonely, formed a friend,
And he,
Was I,
And she,
Had to be her.

And we,
Only laughed cause' we blurred
Moments, yeah we cried,
Wishing it reversed

From beginning to ends
Ends made new beginnings
We began as friends
We noticed every glimpse
Of change or repetition
We cut the purple ribbon,
Apparently red shed

Oh baby, you-
You got what I need,
But you say…
Yeah you say…

Sasha's Nightmare

As the story grew; so did they.

The Good Kid: In today's world anyone could be him. All that it would take is mastering the art of faking the funk, until someone who has already faked the funk, starts to smell the funk being faked. First off, I'll tell you this Good Kid is a tricky individual. He's quite a character. Something close to a Denzel. One with multiple personalities. His strongest trait he carries is definitely his intelligence. He is very ethical. The Good Kid is the type to think twice about his choice of words to impress his audience with strong vocabulary. He knows just about all the right things to say and exactly when to say them. He is the kind of guy that opens the door for his woman. We could see him as the young man that swims across the ocean to prove his love. Or at least that is what he would make you think. You would swear every promise he makes is sincere. Every conversation is meaningful. Every piece of advice given has a twist to it. Others may say he is similar to a two-headed snake. You never know if he is going to strike or tease. That's the "quite a character" trait that I speak of. And as for Sasha, she has no other intention but to fall for a guy like this. Who wouldn't want a young man who portrays himself as everything a woman needs in life? Maybe he is. Maybe he is I. Maybe he is you. Or maybe, you're just anxious to see what this nightmare is all about. Maybe I'll tell you now. Maybe I'll tell you later. Two headed snake talk. Maybe, he is I.

So how is he a nightmare?
I mean, how was I a nightmare?
Because the "Good" only came out when "Good" came in.
I'll explain that later,
Anyway
When no one else would even guess,
Sasha was inspiration.
She was the one breaking the gas pedal
Which kept his heart settled
Which pushed all titles higher than friends
Which put all possibilities to an end
She never liked that.

But he enjoyed her thrill,
He was the one to be revealed,
Standing still, in the middle of second guesses
Through brittle clouds of affection
He fell so swift

The Good Kid,
Always slipping up - here or there,
Always putting buzz in the ear,
Exact words detested
Reel back the purge connected
Turn it into stress,
It's - all a part of the game
Good follows the bad,
Her nightmare was just a phase

There's a good kid,
With a soft kiss,
And a smile that talks majestic,
And a good girl,
With some hood curls,
That had a dominant connection,
A spontaneous complexion,
Of the right mind and the right line,
She liked emcees like Einstein,
That fine wine – was what we never sipped
We missed the cues,
And went on quests - to find out - what love meant

And these are the results.

Gently down the stream,
Merrily, I rowed the boat.
Two engaged in thrills,
It was very difficult,
The cult of personality,
Stabbed her in the throat,
She screamed and blood dripped,
And that's when she awoke.

Do you see the irony?
Do you see what he did?
Do you see that this is just an introduction?
Finding love can fracture how your mind functions,
It's okay to not forget,
Forgiving can be a sin.

And she forgave me.
That was when she hit the nightmare.
She opened her eyes,
"Shhh, listen baby. I'm right here"
She said, "Who are you?"
"I'm right where I desire…"
"I got something for you that can make you feel higher."
This is where she took a sip of poison in her mind.
And that's how love,
Became the sickest drug in her life.

Part One: The Philosophy of a Good Kid

Within
The Sinner
The Art of Self Expression
The Perfect Place for Shade
A Lover's Domain
Cigarette Bud Love
Room Full of Visions
Promise
Dying of Thirst

Within the past few years, I discovered and held onto an ego through the lyrics of one of my favorite artist, Kendrick Lamar. This ego was built in my days of practicing understanding and vision. I began to grow spiritually during my junior year of high school. There was always a connection that I reached when I listened to the lyrics of Kendrick Lamar. This connection changed my perspective on learning. It also changed the way that I began to think, it gave me a desire to learn, and it offered me a burning passion to find answers in life that to some are not so easy to find.

Think of a moment that offered you nothing but confusion at the time but somewhere down the line you found yourself striving to find the purpose. To understand, episodes such as, was an ongoing challenge for me.

The purpose of my confusion was revealed to me when I began writing this chapter. From listening to the lyrics of Kendrick Lamar daily, I grew as a thinker. When I say my purpose was revealed I am referring to how my confusion gave birth to my spiritual growth. What that means is, had it not have been for the things I grew to be confused about in life, I would have never learned how to get through some of the mental battles and obstacles life has thrown at me.

As I would try my hardest to understand the messages in Kendrick's lyrics, I'd catch myself relating to stories that illustrated his childhood. His past inspired me to tell the stories of my childhood. It was kind of like his music gave birth to an ego. That ego to me, is who I call, "The Good Kid." My favorite album by Kendrick Lamar is "GKMC" which stands for "Good Kid M.A.a.D City." This album was a piece of art that spoke to me metaphorically. With Kendrick being one of my favorite rap artist – yes, of all time- I was very proud to use his symbolized character known as "Good Kid" and transfer the similarities he and I share.

Kendrick's story, told throughout his whole album, taught me the importance of understanding and vision. And with that, I give it back to you. Find your understanding. Find your vision. Your vision is what you focus on. It is that 'something' that drives you. And in some ways, you can even say that is what centers you. Eyes open or closed. In your car or in the shower. Find your vision. Then, once you find it, stick to it. Whatever it is that you can relate to on this earth, let that build you. Learn from it. If you can make a connection, with anything, make that connection and use it as another opportunity to learn. Connections are keys to life. They will reveal to you the wrongs and the rights.

Connections present the moment of analysis, before making a decision. Having a connection with something or someone in your time destined on Earth is very essential to building relationships. Connections start within and then they grow to the outside world. If you have not found your vision then you do not know yourself. At least not as much of which you are knowledgeable. So, just as the wise man told Sasha, as she was searching for love, you too, take that advice, "Go! Go find it!"

Thinking outside "the box" can guide you to so many places. Never be afraid to enter what is inside. Sometimes, what is offered by the nature of the outside world is what can guide one to 'see' what is inside. Inside your heart, mind, body and soul. Do not be afraid to walk outside while you are confused. Do not be afraid to learn. Make the connections. If you don't know what inside feels like, how will you understand what goes on outside? Learn yourself first. Learn others second. It all starts *within*.

With that being said, within this next series of poems, "it gets real." These poems, written by "The Good Kid", provide information that will help you understand his intentions throughout his journey. He was born into the world as a very emotional individual in the month of July, also known as Cancer season. He was robbed out of his childhood the day he lost his father at the age of 7. From that tender age he blossomed into a split image. Not one day went by in his life where he did not wonder about what his life would have been like if his father were still around.

The Good Kid learned how to stand on his own. He spent a lot of time observing other people's characteristics. He knew that if he watched a dummy make mistakes long enough, that he would learn to not do what that dummy did. He stayed quiet when everyone was loud. He would stop and study who acted like what when this or that person was near just so that he would understand that persons' true colors. With this skill, he developed into a young man who was pensive in everything that he came in contact with. And that's what made him begin to love himself.

As he grew older, he began falling in love with words. They made him feel smarter. He studied words and used them in small talk conversations to impress people. And boy, let me tell you, he was impressive. Despite the pain he had overcome, he fails to show any remorse towards it. He hides his background in yesterday's treasures, masking himself to portray only one type of image whenever he's in the spotlight. This is was what earned him the nickname "The Good Kid." He had the ability to smile in front of everyone while being at his lowest. He had the mindset that everything happens for a reason and nothing happen for nothing. And that was that. Nothing could break him. Nothing could keep him low. He focused on the meaning behind everything and made sure he would learn the lesson that life was teaching him. He taught himself, through the words and actions of others. He used the positive influences, films, artists, and down to earth people in his life to be inspired.

With that mindset, he took everything he went through and wrote about it. His anger, his passion, his pain, his sufferings, his sacrifices, his love, his discomfort. Everything. He put everything into his writings. So that one day he wouldn't have to speak to explain himself. He figured that if people read his story they would perceive the person that he really is. And just like it happened with him and the words of Kendrick, they would find themselves through that process.

Everything from now on will start falling into place. So stay with me. He is lost. Lost within a world of 'I don't know where to turn, who to turn to, or how to continue progressing. Lost inside of his own world. Where love is gloomy at the eye, and slippery on its slopes. Though each of his actions are for the most part chosen after premeditated thought, he handles adversity well. In his very own personal way, he shares his perspective; not to be judged, but to be understood. Not to be pointed for all wrongs, but to prove that his title may sometimes fail to perfectly match with his self-identity. He tells these stories, to you, for you, so that you, can learn from his mistakes. So that you can get to know his true story.

Have you ever felt so low in life, that when you want to tell someone how you feel, it seems it will never come out right? Most of these poems he wrote were directed to the loved ones he has lost. Those loved ones, he can no longer make connections with physically on Earth. These are dearest episodes in his life that shaped him into the young man that he is today. It's not like many people are out there willing to listen to him speak. So with that being said, here goes nothing.

To: Sasha...

The Sinner

For I know, that I am a sinner, who will one day, commit once more.

As the world keeps spinning
As long as the devil is still living,
Temptation will forever dwell within my eyes.
As long as the look of lust covers the unpurified,
I won't notice the truth within life's lies.

"Sometimes, I need to be alone."

I'm still trying to find, Euphoria.
Reaching, screaming for a foreign destination to flee - to
I'm close,
But blinded by whites and stereotypes,
I'm not racist,
Caucasians don't play,
I just sit and pray and I strain my veins at the neck,
Portraying I'm inept
I kept this flame all to myself,
They left, and I guessed that,

"Sometimes, I need to be alone."

I could feel a difference,
Vengeances aren't mine
But lord, I'm tired of conviction
Condemn the curious listener,
Choosing to look with vision,
Instead of his ears,
Because of this,
I hid, many years from my peers

It's hard to listen,
You don't see - inside of me;
You seek - what's frigid.
You see the wit and the wicked,
You see the little commitment.

What trips me out is-
You don't want to say that I'm a sinner
Just like you,
I look, and see the difference – is,
You don't see what the picture is.

For I know, that I am a sinner, who will one day, commit
once more.

Lord, will you be patient? Will you still give love? Restoring my heart, the more and more that you pour the true love that is overflowing my cup. I know who wants to take my heart to tear it all up. No tears anymore, oh Lord. Send them away. Friends so far drifted away, for the sake of getting wasted. They praise demons in the dosha free basing. Lord help me, find answers, and fall in love with our placement. I've searched many places; I've caught many cases, failing to try and not fail. The only place that I haven't been in this life is hell. Lord, I couldn't tell the difference. I'd listen to the devil and ignore all of your whispers.

I've been to paradise. Oh Lord, and still my greatest vice has to be present. I won't roll the dice. I'll just call you first, I'll heal and serve. I have a purpose Lord. It can be a gift and a curse. But that's my fault, I haven't stood at my dresser to pick that verse, on the 23rd, the 23rd word, the lord is my shepherd. I shall not put life first. First, I shall ask for forgiveness. I sin, but all I really need is a dash of attention, but I'm dashing to the finish line and I'm glad I'm forgetting.

"Sometimes, I need to be alone."

So that I can find you. If I could fly to the moon, and stare out into space, would I find you? My cry is little; I don't believe my smile reminds you, to look back into my soul and smile too. Lord forgive me.

Sometimes I need to be alone
I never wish to ask of you to bring me home
Peace,
Inside of me - Inside of you
I only find,
In the times of need
So will you please have mercy on my mind?

Lord, don't leave me alone.

The Art of Self Expression

And my daddy used to always tell me, that one day it'll burn me out.

Growing up I'd doubt to find reality in that sentence. I wish I
could've seen the vision, of myself in the scenes. Or on scenarios I
have yet to see. I've seen the sticky virus. He passed long eyelashes
to prevent water drips from my eyelids. So that when I close my eyes
in shadows of death, I shall not burn bridges with all due respect.

My father told me, this life would burn me out. Here I am, 17.
Everything left undone, everything he said to me, appeared to be
steering my fear in the philosophy. Chronologically, these are the
steps - that left me here - dwelling in his mockery.

Daddy, hear the angels at night? They're taunting me.

It's been silent in our house, since you left. Can you be the one to
guide me through my very next step? My heart is weak, so it hurts to
say this with my chest. I use my hands in peace igniting the flame
that you placed in me. You called that bravery. I called it my only
option.

*Remember the good kid you raised? They stroll pass, as if they never
saw him.*

On the motherland, they all dream of life inside of coffins.
And you say to be modest,
It's hard playing honest.
Why expect a good kid to be perfect?
It makes no sense.
The pressure from my pen bursts, still hurts,
Lord have mercy, my grandma still cursing,
Praying that I learn,
To earn everything, cause nothing is everything I deserve.
Right or wrong?
I do the good things wrong, and the bad things perfect.
I'm invisible and invincible, I feel I have no purpose.

I promise, I don't mean to confuse a stupid mind on purpose,
But still I confuse myself, thinking I am so worthless.
They call me perfect....

I'm just a good kid

Daddy's smoke from his cigarette came out, 2nd handed,
I caught the flame and lit the pain across my pamphlet.
It's hard trying to balance the actions of being average.

I'm not perfect; I'm just a good kid.

The Perfect Place for Shade

Not beneath Palm trees, nor aside still winds surrounding the ocean
Or near casted worries into the flaws of a perfection
Not with the woman of your fiction dreams - silent screams -
affectionate mourns,
Healing the heart that's been torn, reformed and born again
The perfect place for shade would be in the heart of today

I showered my growing pains, I always felt like a coward.
I did my push-ups in school and started abusing my power.
I slipped and hit my head a couple times for attention,
I was a menace in my head, I lived to be an image,
I wasn't, I was just playing the role of little brother,
Under my covers, I discovered the happiest moments,
As for my brother,
He'd just laugh, because he was older,
Now that he's gone,
I just lay here and search for his odor,
The games been over for years,
But I still hold the controller.

The perfect place for shade was never on the blue,
The perfect place for shade was made by me and you,
The perfect place is a moment we deserve to breathe,
The perfect place was thinking of what he said to me,

Daddy said,

If you lay too close to misery and fate,
Unfortunately you will fade
The only way,
To proclaim honesty
Is falling free to fly away
I just had to find my way
To rest in a lovers domain

A Lovers Domain

This is a story about a good kid, who learned how to love through getting lifted, from the atmosphere of weed smoke that he had no choice to live in, alone in his own mind, he found his own vision, he called his remedies his love, and then learned he fell victim, to realizing his life style was based on blue visions, that blew by, high off contact as you stared in his two eyes, he had blue eyes, not red eyes,

So whenever he flew by
In his scuffed Chuck Taylor's they would amplify - his background
He wasn't the strongest - but never backed down to the dudes on the green-box
He battled his traumas - while beat-boxing
He'd "du-wop du-wop du-wop"
And do the moonwalk
In the kitchen
When it was too hot
To cool off
He is
I

He relied, on true empathy to prove, affection wherever his eyes seemed attracted to,

Seen in the scenes on episodes of his hearts TV screen, as he watches it,

He fails to precede the procedure of being provocative, he's lost within. Mental burdens by the barrier and caught within, reality and imagination, he can't seem-to find the differences.

Feeling the motions of motions inferior,
Mental sit-ups, getting wearier,
In the motions of finding love
He fell off,
He was only curious

A Lover's Domain = A brother in pain

As he writes his words they become assumptions, to whoever dwelled in the past, as drastic lovers. Dragging pulses insane, became impulsive. They made it together in a game called love. A game called love, was rearranged.

He's carrying his own luggage, in abundance, loving nobody, he finds simple theories. In his pamphlet, believing his lover was far away still hearing, the words, but behind them the feelings, behind them curtains, he won't lie, she knows he's hurting. He won't cry. He won't stumble and he won't curse. He closes them curtains, 'cause the spotlight makes him nervous.

If love was truly a feeling, rather an action, the verb looking in the mirror wouldn't matter, Kendrick.

He looks, and forever falls victim, to loving another not paying attention. To himself

In a Lovers Domain; lies darkness in the nights

He never lives to see a change, trapped inside his own mind; his mind relied on pain, on top of pain. It's all a game, he kept on saying. To himself.

I can see the anger;
I can see why his life is wild, like a runaway ranger, you don't see the danger. That's in A Lovers Domain as he mourns for a makeup. You can never see the pain; he sips and is forced to partake of.

I can see the hatred;
I can see that his heart and mind have been constantly played with, you're just a stranger. In the thunder and rain, he tries to obtain to find him some patience, in his mind frame, one rose. It's a mind game, no vase. Turned away from what beauty once was, now all love does is just ache him, to the heart like a bullet with no name. Bang! He's afraid of his placement...

He's just a Good Kid; In a Lover's Domain

Cigarette.Bud.Love.

And may I ask,
Sir, why do you drag?
Lazy eyes, looked optimistic in the past.
You said you needed love.
Then, the needles came, it was cold,
I picked it, I lit it,
I did like you, I licked the smoke.

6 years old,
Passed it to my brother, while my mother,
And father were in a box,
We felt the wave - then I got hot,
He got hot too,
Two brothers on the cigarette bud,
That was my buddy,
The trouble was a symbol of love,
And now I miss him.

I stared at my mother and saw her kiss him.
The bud cycled a lifestyle,
We all learned to live in.

We circled,
Certain to fall through what we were accustomed to,
Two brothers,
Picking it up, uncomfortable
But we hit it.

6 years old,
Never knew diamonds were her best friend
When the night spun,
She turned around a moaned for her night bud.

I was so clueless,
I put it to my lips,
"Yo, JC, how I do this?"
                    "Man, here."
My brother,

Why do you drag?
                "I thought, that when you let go,
                It would soon make you glad.
        Terrance! - You better not - go and tell dad.
            Terrance! You better not go..."

                    I never told.

Room Full of Visions

Do they even remember Sammy's laugh?
It always fell back like a quarterback getting sacked
Looking back into my mental
I don't remember the laugh

Guess he never had anything to laugh about

But something always stood out,
When I jumped into his arms after a long day of work,
Written all over his face, spelled "PROUD"

Sammy, why is it so quiet, inside without you here?

Help me remember your voice,
It's quietly bumping in my ears.
It really isn't my choice,
I want a conversation,
For 10 long years I've been waiting.
Drowning in holographic images in my room full of visions,
You left me in there one night - and that's all I remember.

Didn't even say goodbye, why?
Did you have to leave in that fashion?
Written all over my face, is sadness.

Still the good kid that you raised me to be.
I still the remember when you tied my shoes and untangled me,
From the negatives, in life that were coming my way,
Without a father like you, I wouldn't be,
Who I am today.

I talk to myself, or should I say, to you, like you're physically living,
and that's something to smile about.

But if that's true, tell me why I write you all these poems and you
don't even send me,

One in return, that kind of hurts. You said you would be here. You said that, at very top you would see me there. And I see man, you're at the top. What about the lessons that you taught me? Do I teach my son? Or do I tell him what you said and leave all of his hopes to drop? Do I forget? Do I forgive? So when I'm in your position, I'll slip like yo...

I remember when you would put me on your shoulders and spin me around, like I was at the top of the world. Nothing more important. Not candy or even little girls. It cured my little heart when Sammy made me happy. So how they think I'm happy, when Sammy is gone.

November 30th,
The day I learned to bury
My emotions and quickly set them in place
That evening, my superhero had passed away,
7, stuck in the moment,
Frozen on a hospital bed,
I was hoping,
Doctors were honest the very moment that they told me,

"Don't worry, everything will be okay"
He laid on his death bed,
He laid and a tear shed,
Instead, what's a promise?
When my hero is unconscious
"Everything will be alright" they said.

I remember the hug saying goodbye,
Believing you were alive,
And later, you'd somehow come back home.
After all these years, they finally told-
Me, that you were in a coma,
Forcing oxygen within the space of room in your lungs
That very day, two then equaled one.

You know why I never call this place home,
They've been growing apart, while I've been growing so close,
Closer to you, I'm older

This life is so much colder
So much to bear on my shoulders,
Father don't close the doors that were open.

Is it my vibrant memory that you closed? All these years I've been
visioning fantasizes I suppose. What comes around in the circle will
one day close. So tell me why is it silent, though it is loud, what you
show?

Sammy,
Have you felt how I felt,
Since you crept to the moon?
Or have you really even left the room?

I picture you smiling your pictures grasp my attention.
I've been smiling at the simple resemblance,
I remember,
The laugh of Sammy Carter
On purpose
It hurts this Good Kid
But it can't make him feel worthless, anymore.

Promise

"Just promise me you'll tell this story when you make it big,
and if I die before your album drop I hope…"
–Kendrick Lamar

That when the champagne bottles come out
Souls of demons pouting
Will rise and shout in joy right on top of the mountain,
Promise, that you will not forget me
Look, I found a penny
Lucky side up,
I'm hoping that you hear me,
Don't fear me, keep them eyes up,
Be one to forgive me.

When Mary Jane minds sit on clouds
Then, come down,
With fuzzy minds and hearts that reflect frowns
Promise, that you will-fly-without me
I can see you soar,
Only because you doubt me
Be trustworthy.

When the puzzle that we make,
Suddenly breaks to pieces
And life no longer tastes like the berries and peaches
Promise the kid, you will-believe it
Promise that you will-be-
Intriguing

When my mind goes to sleep,
And I can't seem to find myself
And you catch me with backpacks full of needles and belts
Promise that you'll be-there-to cleanse me
Promise that you will-not-forget me
Promise that your heart-will-forgive me
Promise,
That you'll sing in high praises,
My name

Not the wicked angels' - true guardians
Lord knows, I promised them,
One too many promises,
I promise to sing,

Christine: Sammy

Dying Of Thirst

Give me a promise,
Infatuated with death,
And dreams to sin large
Dreams of living free,
Behind Americas' barbed-wire
Through steel bars and locked hands
Bowed heads with black hoodies on
Abroad from home of the brave
As slaves, we are Trayvon,
Well, I know I am

Is it good that I'm so tired of runnin?
Tired of tumblin?
Tired of feeling life is amounting to nothing?

Promise me happy endings,
But renege the beginning
Lie, to mirror divinity
I've been addicted to promises,
Materialistic remedies,
I swallowed them.
In love with weekends,
It brings the freedom
Hands on the clouds,

"Hello, Lisa. What's up Aaliyah?
Pac, pass me the crown"

I'm looking for water,
So out of breath-breathing
Can you lead me - to lead them? So we can,
Stop drinking.
Is it alright, to be, so low?

In the depths of solitude,
Living life solo,
Where you can't handshake-
Holding on to the word "HOPE"
Just go slow...
And solo, in the depths of solitude

To the point where you'd ask God to not bother you

You got this
But the truth is you're lost in…
Deprivation

Is it good to be taking this the wrong way?
Take advantage of word play,
Okay?

"Is everything okay?"

You may - hide from the truth,
Or you may, think that you're hiding
But you're just lying to yourself,
Slowly dying of thirst,

You may search to find proof
Or find the evidence in you
And feel untrue
Though you know the glimpse hurts

And if it hurts,
So be it
The angels told me truth hurts
And if that works to stir your mental
I guess - you know you've been hurt
Before

You walk away from Jesus
You can't take pain anymore
And you pour, all of your, love down the drain…
Hoping for the change

For someone to hear your cry
As your voice starts to strain itself
Veins pop from your neck-and
Nobody can help, you

Even if you were to-call his name
You feel-because-you went astray
He won't answer the day-you-call
As if he hates you; but he will never forsake you
Brought you in and he can take you
Out - but he forgave you
Way before you dreamed of the angels
Remember when he saved you?

When surface = many different angles
From thoughts you caved in – can you cradle your thoughts?

You're still dying of thirst

Losing your memory

Not remembering

The blessings you have been blessed with

Too busy mentioning

All the times you've been tested

You never forget to mention

The times you fell victim

It's hurting - because you get it
I wish you could've got it in your pocket,
Gaining profit,
Way before these tears became solid

Part Two: Blinded by Venom

Poison

Should've Known

Why Can't I get you out of my head?

Too Young

Amusement Park

Thursday Nights

Phone Call

Sophisticated

Silly of Me

Let's Have Some Fun
But
Losing Love
Lovely Sight to see
Fiji Flow
The Fight
We were once a fairy tale
Little Did They Know
Break Up to Make Up
In the Night
It Never Rains
I Don't Mean It
Hold On
Sighs Of Depression
Can't Cry
Let Me Explain

I could never remember where I lost it for sure. I just remember where I first found it. I was lost; but it was present. Then, I became present, and watched it slowly disappear. The lights flickered on and off. The touch was cold, then soft. The vibe was strong, then gone. And before I knew it, I was lost again.

One day, I was in Sasha's mind, writing with confusion yet so much ease. When writing as if I were her, it didn't hurt as much. She never hurt the way that I hurt. As me being her mentally, I failed to see things clearly. The next thing I remember, I was sitting in a dark corner, finding love, within myself. I never thought that it would be in my darkest moments alone that I would find the real me. Once she and I had separated, that's when I found it. Which is common between two lovers, right?

Once you leave that special person, it seems as if you learn so much more about yourself that at one point you were blind to understand. That person, should be the one who drives you to find love within yourself before you search for it in them. That person, should be the one who inspires you to grow to learn yourself. If you are not simply growing as a human being, by giving more than you ask for, then you are receiving very little or close to no personal gains in life.

God gives to those who give. If you do not give, you shall not receive in the greatest manners available. He or she who does not give, settles. During my first years of middle school, I was just learning how to find "*it*". Find what? Just learning how to find love. I don't remember where I lost it; but I do remember where I first found it. Finding it, did not take all the years of my life. Learning to accept "*it*" for what it truly is, instead of what the world tells (me) "*it*" is, was what took me years to accomplish. Not just for me, but mostly for everyone. It wasn't hiding in someone else. It wasn't waiting for me at the altar in a white dress. It wasn't even too far out of my grasp. It was inside of me. It still is.

As for you, there "*it*" is too, stimulating your mind and waiting for you to catch it, love. Be quiet, and mute everyone in your presence. Stop and listen, yes, there "*it*" is. Love. Let me tell you a little story, about love...

I remember listening to the smash hit 90's song by Bell Biv Devoe, "Poison" as a kid. My mother would play it loud on the radio all the time. And of course, I'd be in the backseat jammin'. It didn't matter how many people were in the car, it didn't matter if I wasn't feeling good, that song was played, and most definitely jammed to. It wasn't until I was in middle school until I actually knew what the song meant.

Around freshman year, I finally had the concept of the song down pat. Everything had become so clear. I remember it as if it all happened yesterday. "If I were you I'd take precaution." The signs were all there. I was just too attracted to flow. Too sucked into the rhythm, the beat, the way the bass dropped and sped back up. The only thing is, when it finally hit me, the bass never dropped. Everything was louder. Everything was vibrant. Every mouth was open. Every heart was silent. Except mine.

And here is where it all truly begins. Remember when I told you, *"Here's the treat, your eyes are my paper, these lines are the paint, and I am the artist, painting the picture?"* Well, here's the picture. Here is where I need you to go from reader to traveler. I'll do all the guiding. Try not to get lost in the words. Don't get distracted by trying to figure out what and who. Remember, we are still trying to figure out what this thing called "love" really is. This chapter will take you down "First Avenue", wherever that is in your mind, let's go! Take a deep breath.

Think of the last time you woke up in the middle of the night because of a nightmare. Think of those chilly nights where you would stare at the ceiling in the dark and try to find a way out of "no way". Think of being trapped in darkness and forcing yourself to live in a beautiful mindset. Think of walking all alone on a rainy night in the forest. Dark Spruced Forest, where the snakes hiss louder than the little voice in your head. Think of that girl who is crying herself to sleep right now. Think of papa, who was a rolling stone, and try to understand why he spends more time with his bottle than he does with his family. Think of having so much space that it feels like no space at all. Think of kindergarten crushes.

Remember that special person each year in school that you "wanted" for so long? Think of why you still remember them, and think about the feeling that they once gave you. Think about love on any aspect you can remember. Think about it? Think about you.

"Excuse me, Terrance, what is this POISON that you speak of? Where did that come about?"

Let me start by saying that everything bad that enters the human mind, is POISON. Everything considered bad, as in things that have the power to make us unhappy. All the heartache, the affairs, the fights, depression, tears, storm outs, lonely nights etc. That's the poison. That's what can truly kill a person. The poison has the power to make one believe they amount to nothing. It's strong enough to knock somebody so low, that they would rather die. *Is it alright to be so low, in the depths of solitude?* So low that in the midst of that lowliness, you can only hold onto so many things before you let go. Have you been there before? If so, you've been sipping the poison.

"Oh, okay. I get it! So, Terrance, Where does Magic Land come from? What does Magic have to do with love?"

Oh! Right! You see, Magic Land, can be described as an imaginary state of mind. In this state of mind, the perspective of love is illustrated by lustful wishing and fantasized satisfaction. Universally, Magic Land can be broken down as "puppy love". The Good Kid and Sasha are taking a journey in their years of Magic Land together.

Actually you are too, right now. This is the land of imagination, where love has expectations. These expectations make people forget to search to find a true connection within themselves while looking for love. I once heard:

You cannot love someone else; until you have learned to love yourself.

Most of the people in my generation believe that love is dead. I asked a young girl one day,

"What do you think about love?"

She said, "It's losing its meaning nowadays."

"Tell me why?" I said, trying to get a good answer out of her.

"People use it so freely. Therefore, I don't believe in it."

I stopped and tried to understand what she meant by that. I admit, I was confused for a bit but understood what she was getting at. So I asked her,

"You say 'it' like you know what 'it' truly is. What is it? Have you experienced it?

"Mmm, I thought I did."

"Exactly! We've all thought. I've thought I found love a thousand times before I truly did. So you're telling me, you *thought* you were in love, but you weren't?

"Yeah."

"So what were you in?

"I don't know."

"You say you weren't in love, and you don't know what you were in. Do you know what love really is? Do you know true love? Or are you living in Magic Land?"

If you don't know,
What you feel,
When you're feeling it,
Then, it's not real.

Magic Land is the thought of "love" in our minds. It's the watered down thought of what many people consider real love to be. Let me be the first to tell you, love isn't always holding hands. Love isn't always happy faces and good vibes. Love comes with a dark side.

Love comes with disagreements and disappointments. Love is not a "Relationship Goal". Love is not a Cinderella story with long white dresses and diamond rings. Love is not what is always broadcasted on the outside. True love is formed on the inside. It is deeply inside of you. Love can take years to find. It takes a person to be willing to sacrifice themselves to receive true love in their life. Love is not just an abstract thing. It is more than just words. Loving yourself can do no harm to anyone. When you are one who has self-love, you are no danger nor threat to anyone. With self-love you have courage, strength, and power. Don't be afraid to use it.

Have you ever met someone who is always down? Someone who stays in a dark shade of emotion? I guarantee you it is because they lack (some sort) of self-love. He who loves himself has the strength to love everyone. That is why you must learn to love yourself before you love others. This brings me to the example of a happy person. Now, have you ever known a person who is always happy? Someone who has a light in them that always seem to shine? Even in the dark times of life, that someone always makes you smile on the inside, or if not you, someone else. Well, that person is filled with love. Self-love.

Having self-love doesn't make you necessarily **better** than anyone. It more often holds the power to get a person through situations that for those who lack self-love would have a harder time getting through. Some people say money makes the world go around. I say, love makes the world go around. We can do so much more with love. We can give love, spread love through our home communities, teach about love to those who are unaware of its importance, and last but not least, we can practice loving ourselves.

One of our biggest problems is that we have placed expectations on love. Love should have no expectation. If you have to expect it soon or later you're going to reject it. Accept love as it is. You are only making your journey worse when you add expectations. I've learned to give without expecting anything in return.

When you do so, you gain much more. You notice and appreciate the blessings that are given to you. Some people expect affection, empathy, wealth, praises and to be drenched in love.

As lovers, we do not need so many large doses. We need to stop and be grateful for the little things that we enjoy so much while we are in love. We must enjoy our breaths given to us by God. Inhale and exhale and strive to find harmony with God. Once you connect with God, you are connected with all of his blessings. The more you spend time acknowledging God for what he provides and controls; the more blessings he will give you. Your connection with God isn't as scary as it sounds, God is within you. He is the little voice in your head that tells you to do the right thing when you think of doing the wrong things. God is your guide. He is the one that wants the best for you.

We all have another voice in us, a voice from the world, a voice that only wants the worst for us. Listening to that voice is what distracts us and keeps us away from our connection with God. You can be led by both of these voices. God gives you a choice to listen to either voice. The life you live when you are connected to God is a life that is spiritually and mentally rich. Listening to the other voice will have you tricked, misused, and you will lose your knowledge of self. You will lose your self-love and it will be harder for you to be mentally strong when life gets rough. If you want to live an enriched life and experience true love, find God and keep him close to you. He has your back, and he will give you the true desires of your heart.

Keep your eyes open, here's the key. I said, keep your eyes open, here's the key…

Poison

Driven out of my own mind,
That's why it's hard for me to find
Treasure, super glued in my head
Oh my, oh my, oh my, it's poison...

It's just, one who got caught alluring thick hips and a smile
Searching for the shortcuts in a mile
Never strong enough to turn away from
Miss her, kiss her, and love her
Never taught to worry for another

What is poison?
A substance with capabilities of kissing me
But inside of my heart, slowly killing me
When introduced into the mind, body and soul
How so, do you cure?
Is this pure?

Are these fantasies? Sophisticated back-breaking fascinations?
Because love is so,
You know...

We fall for what's portrayed
We hide within our faces,
Two roses and naked
Last bid, last choice, last coin,
Oh my, oh my, it's poison

When I squeeze you tight,
Does it hurt your little heart?
I know we aren't stars,
But somehow we see the light

Never trust a thick curve and a grin,
Correlated with lust,
In the end, the appearance is a plus,
(That is) correlated with sins
Reunited with love

Just, for pleasure

Due to the indefinite, dead thick,
Fantasies stick,
And we're stuck sinking when,
We sip,
This poison.

Should've Known

They gave him many mixed signals,

"Don't do it"

He heard, but was too stubborn to listen
I suppose he was numb by the taste of the kisses
He felt that message
She cheated with his so called best-friend,

So he dialed 10 digits in his phone…

"Now I peep why you always smelt like his cologne,
Why you always ask about his goals,
You asked me where he goes,
You asked about, the things I doubt,
While diving into phones,
I dive, into your mind - only to swim alone.
I cry when you're not home,
But when you come back - you still hope – hoping for a comeback.
Who even cares, if you just had been there and done that?
Not me!

I see why you're always texting
Stressing over what's best for you,
I never learned that lesson
All those nights with no reply
Breaking down the lies
You know you're wrong,
You mastered that disguise
Lying in the bed-steady lying
Crying on the inside, you give but can't take.
You've entered pretty late,
Messing up the icing on red velvet cake
Taunting with tactics
Nibbling in cookie jars for satisfaction
Mama said "Hope"
So I don't, look backwards.

Once I - rewind to times
When love was just a word inside

77

My world,
Pretending to feel the *feeling-*
Picture the kid
Brokenhearted smiling in an image
The only thing - missing,
Was true love all night long
I should've known.

Why can't I get you out of my head?

It's like I hold on to the good times,
But never do it on purpose.
Like, I hold onto your merchandise
Without it getting purchased.
This love was never purchased.
How you flirt with pleasure
By touching the places that make me nervous?

You know, I know that you already heard this…
Before, so I wouldn't be surprised if you ignore
My heart the way it likes to pour
Sinking like water upon the shores
I get close,
Then closer feels like it's further to more
What more should I do?

Fall back, back step?
Back to life
Back to statues of present time
Solitary confinement within my brain cells
Can't stand the fact that you came…
Well,
You came well.

I hold these valuable memories
Regardless if you're hearing me
If I get through misery
There's no remedy instilled to wipe the tears I shed
For you,
I fail to get the blood off my hands.
On blue
Days, dazing always made us feel bad
So instead, we learned to live through fantasies in my head

Why can't I get you out?
I spit it from my mouth,
But never figured out how,
Sick I was,

It's crazy, now all I feel is down.
Should've listened
Mama said love is the sickest drug around

Too Young

You're never too young to learn,
For your own advantage,
First, we flirt
Third, we jerk it off.
Wait a second.
It only takes a minute for smiles to peak
You're never too young
To teach the sprung
How to spring

We were never too young,
Just too stunned, in loving.
If you got it, I got it,
We knew where we were coming-from.
Simple lessons helped us progress into better persons
We were two, one in a millions,
But two different versions
Was it okay?

Do the youngest learn it all today?
Or tomorrow,
Does the sorrow burn and everything decays?

Never too young to be afraid,
Or never too old, should I say either.
With some guidance,
We can find our way through noises in the silence

Find out what this love means,
To each, it's always different.
The fact is, we yearn for satisfaction,
We mind the masses too much,
So of course, the world matched us,
A four letter word,
Formed together forcing internal crashes.
When we crash,
We're then too old to move backwards.

No insurance,
Too young to keep up the paste,
And too many lack endurance.
Never too young to learn,
To love, doing so,
Our hearts will burn.
I didn't know, you had to be old, to teach.

Amusement Park

Your rollercoaster was never one to play with. Like an unpredictable cadence. Your vibe, can be oh-so-very hectic. Good, bad, ugly, sick, etcetera. But, whatever. I mean, who cares that I was afraid of Ferris Wheels. Wedding rings and baby girls walking in high heels, was only a thrill to you. Who knew that when the sky went from bright blue, to a light purp, you would be smiling; and I would be hurt. It was never even my intention to be the one, who's hitting that? I might as well just hit it too. You feel the wrath? Let's wrap it up? We can fold it up and box it back. But, how about I just get back, to the poem.

Stuck on this Ferris wheel
Alive, I'm not dreaming
Forgetting about how they feel
No one can ever make me feel
The way you did
Past tense
Now, I'm coming down

Entering a town
With popcorn shells, fairy tales, and cotton candy
Mad love has found me
It can only surround me, here.
You hear that? No.

What shall I scream for?
Run away, run away
Escape to the sky swings
Let me scribble our names in a cloud
I may never reach the ground; what a wonderful feeling

One step, silent, keeping the stress away.
Second step, finally, stealing my breaths away.
Third step, she awaits, we create,
Chaos.
Fourth step, forfeit the grind and then we,
Take off.
To my right, stress.

To my left, second guesses.
Time? Clock ticks – it's 10:55

Never lost a step, never felt I was affected
Until I heard,

"Attention all... The Amusement Park closes at 11."

Thursday Nights

Sometimes you hate to leave somebody,
Grab my body,
Slowly taunt me,
Cold winds taught me,
This, is everything.

We were both 17,
5:17, it was.
The sun was gone,
The vibes were strong,
The rides were long,
The right was wrong,
But it, was everything.

Not Wednesday,
But Thursday nights,
When lips greeted another,
Hunger,
Became addictive,
And that became ambition,
And we could never lose,
If the two, of us were in this,
Together.

Warm winds came when you smiled,
Too wild,
Through crowds, blue clouds,
Grey skies,
Wait why?

Thursday,
Souls swing; hearts play
Gold leaves decay
A tour is eight more,
Trips through the same door,
We came? Sure.
Before, it was too lame
Too late on Tuesday,

Winds strong on Wednesday,
They calm down on Thursday,
We mistake the light,
Pipe down,
Enjoying thrills
Right?
Now.

Phone Call

I got a phone call from a friend
(I toss and turn)
Vibrations of my phone made me stop and grin
(I wipe my eyes) to realize just who it was
"It's her," I smiled. And no, not her.
Herrrrr! (Winks)

Silence when I say hello. So it must be urgent. I mean, she must be
hurting.
So I finally ask her, "What's the matter?" Silence.
Struggling spitting words out, she sighs,
And cries, "T, he keeps telling me lies."
(I just yawn and rub my eyes)
Not realizing, just how much she needs me

Time flies, I find comfort on my pillow. She lets out a mellow
"Hello?"
"Yea, I'm here, let it out, and breathe." She went on, "Well, I caught
him cheating again. And of course, I'm walking towards seeing this
is the end," I said. "I think you need to slow down. Trust me. Let
him be the one to lose and be left unlucky. You really can't erase the
feeling of feeling like nothing. Even if it was something, learn to let
it go, honey."

"I remember, he said he'd never hurt me…"

"Here's what you do. Give him back no mercy. Give him water if he
asks, when he's thirsty. But when he offers, you have to think -
about the burning - girl in the mirror,
Is he still trustworthy?"

"But, you know, I just love him, and..."

"Yeah, I hear it all the time. So explain to me the reason that he always makes you cry. Explain to me the reason that you're never on his mind. And, call me back the moment that you figure out why. Funny how we make it to these places in relationships, higher than the heavens once, in seconds on the pavement. It's crazy at the paste, you find comfort in this place, tears rolling down your face. And, you still say you love him."

But when you don't know what to say,
I can always pray for you.
As God creates another way for you.
Learn better ways to - make yourself available
Take some time to reflect – it could take a day or two

Maybe you,
Can teach me, lessons
It's not all about perfection
You truly do learn the most
When stuck in your mistakes.

Sophisticated

Just searching for a girl who's sophisticated
And oh, how she is
The way she makes my head spin
It should be a crime

From smiles to grins
From fails to wins
From beginning to end
Never in a day was it easy to win, you over

All it takes is one moment - to make up for it
One smile, then I'll adore it
Impatient
I fail to - turn away from your sweet fragrance
You're so sophisticated

So discombobulated,
But face it I'll just embrace it
Disconnected
Wrapped around your neck like a necklace
Never take it the wrong way
But let's go the long way
In the still of the night,
You, steal my mind
Forget my pipe, near your thighs
I want the intellect
Forget what's in between,
Though, it feels right when we intersect.

I'm lost in your soft touch,
This feeling doesn't cost much.
But it's all worth the amounts I hurt.
I hate it, while it's making sense.
Making sense is money.
Success is what buzzes,
You just happen to be my honey.
You're sophisticated.

I put the ruby roses in baby blue vases, for you.
I guess I'm the fool,
In your smart world
Mama said - *one day*
I will find myself a smart girl

Silly of Me

To think that you…
Could take the pain away
And to believe that your smile would never fade
So that I would stay
And remain inside your world of intimacy

Silly of me - silly of me
To even care
To run my fingers through your hair
As you closed your eyes, and tried to hear
Not spare, the little love we share
Silly

Oh love - oh love
Stop! With your silly ways
That send me to a maze
Confused - with you - trapped deep in a phase
I'd rather be - no other place
Unfortunately, this love fades…

And when it does,
I'll just be another fool - who fell for the trap
One who deserves the biggest slap
To the face - without feeling sad
I knew - it wouldn't last
This time - I can't get mad
I'm a fool,
I tried to keep - what I never had.

Oh love, oh love
Stop making - a fool - of me
I'm not used to this pain,
This is new to me.
I'm asking you

"Don't do this to me."
After all,

You're the only one influencing me.
When you call.

Let's Have Some Fun

I'm just up
Like the night before the first day of high school
Floating like I'm yearning on a hot air balloon
But only when you give me the blues
Say you walk around picking up clues
Missing this cues
I write haiku's; you misuse the word - affection

When you're going on and on and on,
About how every little step we take is wrong,
And how everything we do isn't fun
Then you pause,
Only - because I cut you off
Just to scream let's have some fun
Let's time machine ourselves back to when we had fun
And let's become

Two, in this lovely universe
Flap our wings to the moon
We don't need to rehearse
Let's just go!
Leave your wallet and your purse
I remember when you first
Told me, that you would sacrifice
Much, just to stay in my life
So leave it all to be with me?

I'm not asking for a wife
But while I'm young, just make it fun
When we're done... let's laugh and smile
Quicker than a bullet racing out of the barrel
Don't make a wide path narrow
Let's just have some fun

But

You don't want to have fun
Giving me the eye, like I'm the crazy one
When I'm just suggesting
Ideas to what you're frequently requesting
You don't want to get up off your…

But, you're the one always accusing
Assuming, there's that one wrong thing that I'm doing
Always stressing,
Yelling out, I'm the one who's losing, your love.
And I'm the one who always ruins…
You would, be the one to talk about losing love

When, you're the one who's so dramatic
In my ear, filling me with anger, it's fantastic
You would be the one to talk about losing love
Soon, you'll be missing out on this love, for good

This is for the lovers,
Who live the back-to-back argument-
Right and wrong,
GET AWAY!
NO! YOU STARTED IT!

Leave me alone,
Go talk to those…

Give me some space, fights.
To knockout and wake up only to realize…

Just how much fun it all is,
When you're in love,
Sipping the poison.

Losing Love

Dear You,
Yes, you know who you are...

I'm losing my love to an unknown
Love that has constantly grown
A silent bond, in my hearts pond
I'm sick and tired of leaking on
And speaking on, this unknown love
I'm done!

I'm losing this love,
Like a wife without her hus-
Band-Aid unto the heart without a pulse
Without a beat, without a lung
Breathe poetry
To wake me up, I'm losing blood
Losing love and giving up

No belief in "trust me"
Losing, like a leprechaun without luck
Like a fiend without the fix
Like a mind without the flesh
I feel like a skeleton
With a pen inside my hand
Writing so elusive,
Spilling everything I've been losing, you.
Said,

The red after the blue, is sexy soothing.
Feelings, Emotions, Hope,
I'm moving, each duty,
Each promise, these responses,
Mock the problem, mama help,
But mom can't solve this.

She say love is toxic
Eliminate the nonsense,
Pick the poison, pick the profit

Cause when it all runs out…
Ya' better have something to show for it.
Ya' better do more than just adore it.
I know you abuse it, I know you abuse it
And soon enough,
You'll wake up, and realize that you are losing.

Lovely Sight to See

I cannot focus
Feeling hopeless
And I cannot say
That I have faith
To end this phase or pray through days
What a shame…

That I can't help but lay
In disbelief,
Making you think that I'm okay
When I'm just resting out of place

Forever in my ear
Yes, my mind is drifted clearly
Never focused
Just ignoring
When you pour
On those stairs
I stare
At the doors before your pupils, and adore

Skeptical to,
Where - I can't prove a point anymore
I slide coins through the slot machine
To gamble for the mighty green
I would need, for ends to meet

For you to smile,
I'll walk a sorrow hectic mile
Because your soul is full of greed
Strutting lanes with tons of speed
While life is at its slowest peak
You bring me to my lowest peak
No one seems to notice me,
At all. None, at all.

Where did time fly - to provide for me?
You're in denial, I can see

You love, but still you lie to me
Rationalize and justify
To compromise what can't be beat
You and I,
The irony
Snap a flick and tell me,
It was all a lovely sight to see.

Fiji Flow

At least we fell in love with something cute,
You all alone force a torch; so freely.
You played my heart as if it were a flute,
Glance at dots, connected, you complete me.
Love, with intentions of gratification
Oh, how you grab the taste of fruits at once,
Our truth spilled after initiation
Oops, we only did it so that we can dunce.
Cameras gave us cancer, we kissed the lens,
Kissing through the end, baby, it was real.
Love was never thick, neither did it cleanse
Sunsets, made us destined to get a meal.
Too fast to be addictive in the time.
I kept fractions of love impacted through the vibe

And through my eyes,
This is what you want to be,
Wondering,
If wandering would be the proper cause for me
Or affection, infected inside our property
This home - is - not a home, monogamy
Probably, flossed before the lottery
Mixtures of miscues and misses
The mistress missed you.

Which was never none of my business
Flicks finally clicked in
It was never your vision
But I saw it, it blew by so blue,
At least we fell in love with something cute.
Wouldn't cha say?
I guess this is,
Where we fall and slip on the pa...

It's,
Not always a pretty ending.
It's,
Not always the shinning penny
That falls far away,
From a wish like Hardaway.
Not everyone's two cent,
Equals a solid pay.
That's just the harder way, we learned it.
That's how the water play, we deserved it.

The Fight

And it's funny that you never find a way
To escape.
Can we ever find the brightside?
Or fight the feeling
We're feeling,
You feel me?

Afraid, for every time we make
Up fantasies, dancing free,
Reality in our minds becomes harder to find

So how will I treasure
Our past if it never
Happened, or never lasted?
And after repairs
We cruise then crash when
We mix, we don't match then
From there it's all tragic
Trying to work my magic
Trying to fix the cracks within our pavement
I seem to crave it,
Will you stick with it?
Whenever I should erase it?

I just grasp the things I want
When they call my name, they taunt
Playing hide and seek
Leaving me hopeless
In dreams,
I can only hope this
Dream won't last forever
It was never exciting
I just hope,
One day,
My mind will stop fighting,
Itself.

We Were Once a Fairy Tale

Once upon a time we were
One, but never again
Not too long ago
We were just the best of friends
So desperate

For that one thing
That we'd search to find
Took advantage of, then wondered why
When the vibe left, we would go right
On about our business

What happened?
It all comes back in a blink
Of an eye
Shutting facts in our past
Still wondering why
Again, we'd begin to not express how we feel
But imagine how it would feel
If this fairytale was real

From the spark in your eyes
And every single time you smile
In the meantime,
Mean times turn nice for a moment.
Golden souls with arms out
And no one has time for holding
I guess we moved on from those days
And adapted to all alone days

Before realizing the 4 letter word
Was near our atmosphere, we began to speak the words
Into our daily life, before the first time that I met you
I knew, that we once were a fairytale, I left you
Locked inside a place where nothing can make me forget you
More than just a fantasy
Fanning me near my temple
I wish that we can smile again and make it through these days soon

Make it through the day, noon, night, and sunrise.
I left because you left, and left misery in my mind
I left, because you left, right when I asked you to be mine

We were once, "something"
And now…

Little Did They Know

Such a pretty picture they said
But little did they know
That we both
Truly don't, love our pictures in the mirror

Such a lovely smile they all said
When little did they know
The pain behind all smiles
Which we are great at faking

So real, they all said
But little did they know
Those images portrayed half of the time
We put out just for them

Such a good relationship they said
But little did they know
The number of days we wished it would end

"You have pretty eyes" they all said
But little did they know
All the tears that we shed
And all the times that we begged
Them to stop flowing in bed

And little did they know,
All the times I cried.
How hard I tried, to make her smile
To love, when I should've never - loved,
Shoving her, I didn't know,
My actions weren't clever

Little did they know, that
Nothing good lasts forever
Around here
In the essence of tragic,
Land of the magic
Where going forward feels the same - as moving backwards

Break Up to Make Up

That's a game for two; so they say
Who said I wanted it to be that way?
All of a sudden
I have no say so

So, we break up to make up
We interact to stay up
Argue and fuss
Barge through another's space, daily, we just
Get on each other's nerves
Until the knife cuts deep and baby gets her feelings hurt

As for mine, they hurt as well
But I will never tell, you
For the simple fact that you're a female
I don't think you care for details
Or all I'm talking about
Often, the words I utter, come out
Traveling, from one ear
Out the other

So I'd rather suffer, and not tell you a word
Never admitting I'm sad
In the morning I'll be glad
That I woke up from your text
Smile and hop right out of bed
Suddenly I'll forget
About the fight that we just had

And later on, you start to fuss
So here it comes again
We break up to make up
And fight it till' the end
Honestly, I can feel us coming to an end
And I can't even pretend
That I'm happy anymore.

In the Night

We stand in the heart of this cul de sac
Where it seems that there is no path for us to turn back
Under the street lights beaming down on hardened tar
Patiently waiting
For the moment in the making
To come

Eternity flew by
In the still of the night
While I meditated my mind
Your pure heart I couldn't find
Until, you shed bitter tears

Then after pain you came to me
And there I found myself
Gaining peace and asking for your help
All the burdens from my chest
Disappeared as we wept
Then we slept
In total peace
All because you showed me
That you cared, when I said…

I love you so
And never wish to let you go
When suddenly you start to show
That you care
For the both
Of
Us.

It Never Rains

It's been so long
Since the last time that I made you smile
From my arms protecting you

So come close if you are cold

Allow me to take this stand,
Pause in the middle of the brittle love dance
And appreciate what you always take advantage of
It never rains in Southern California, Sasha.

So when you feel the need to tell me,
You need someone to love,
Don't you dare over think,
And let coaxing defeat

Just let it be

Let your words come down
Replacing precipitation
In Magic Land
It never rains
So we should be okay

You don't need umbrellas to cover your mane
Where we tend to leave our rights wide open
Waiting on May
On just this side of town
Water never drained on my face
We never opened our mouths to be quenched by the rain
We swallow poison

We make up due to fights
Take off on flights
Of amazing excitement

And without a doubt, we like it

Enjoying the warm hugs we give in this weather,
Loving each other's presence,
Cherish holding my hand.
It never rains in Magic Land,

Sip the poison slow,
And watch how smooth you feel when we go - dance

Love taps out of misery,
Tomorrow you'll be missing me
Don't skip a kiss or miss a beat
Remember me,
I am gentle.

I Don't Mean It

I may say that I'm done,
Maybe make you feel unloved,
But I don't mean,
To be mean, keep my secrets?

I just might lie for your sympathy,
Walk you into misery,
I need you to hear my cry
Don't turn your back and spin from me.

Maybe, I'm in a bitter dream,
Between a rock and a hard place
Squeezing in the middle,
Only, you may have to fit too.

I'm making sacrifices to survive,
And you're invited.
You can tell me all your secrets
I'll keep quiet.

If you subtract diamonds and pearls
On what's already gorgeous,
I hope you'll find the Lord's gift.
Bloom to majesty,
So in the end,
You'll still be looking after me.

Being the key to your happiness is as important
Even though you don't always see
Gentle episodes are for me.

Can you keep those quiet places in the past?
Stored away, learning how to forgive me for my actions?

I may say that I don't love you.
But still, I'm dreaming of you.
Put downs?
We hit those until delirious,
I'm curious, the way I did it, can you still forgive it?

I never meant to love you through revenge
But I did it,
And I'm here,
Please hold tight to my golden spirit.

Hold On

Hold on, here it is
Not again
Me being sorry
For everything that you did

I can't believe
I actually believed
Your fake cry,
Your sweet lie
That meek smile, so dirty.
Burning all over,
Again, to only hurt me.

Hold on
Wait a second, minute, hour, day, week…
I'm weak,
Your foot against my chest,
Keeping me down,
I'm infatuated with death,
In disparity's town

I found your weakness
And beat it,
I know I told you…
I didn't mean it
But oh, how I mean, every single-
Word bleeding, from my head to my tongue
We went from "I'm ready" to "I'm done"
Freely.

Meaning, I lied…
So I'm sorry for mixed feelings
You should've never hit me,
Right where it hurts.
Revenge is what I seek
But I can't hurt, you.
Is it worth it?
Hold on,

I'm clearing up - what has always been blurred

Because I know that you'll come back, vicious.
And I know this surely isn't, love.
Lustful wishing can kill a spirit, huh?
I should've known.

Sighs of Depression

The only thing left, are sighs of depression
Because I couldn't learn how to learn my lesson
And I couldn't learn to not stress, on stress
Couldn't realize that life is life…
Regardless

If you like it or not,
Eventually, you'll hit that speed bump
Followed by the consequences of wanting more than enough
Then, you settle for less
And start to reminisce, the blessings, the presents, the messages
We could have been, something.

I wish I would've listened,
And never made dumb decisions,
Never cared for the mistress,
It was never my intension.
To end up in a chair, running my fingers through my hair
Asking "Baby, why is life not fair?"

Now, do you care?
That my sigh was caused by the glare,
From the man, in the mirror
Power punching, as I stared.

Finding out the bare minimum of reasons why,
I reminisce letting go of my sins,
With gentle sighs

Uh, maybe I'm just tired, of nonsense,
The person who caused this,
Or illuminated ways to shine, in this time
We? Flawless.

Everyone?
Drops at the pentacle of the problem,
No one near me will hear me,
And no one helps me stop this!

Sigh

Can't Cry

Sometimes the sunshine will quickly form to rain
The ones who say they love you, bring pain
And tomorrow, still will not be promised
So you can honestly, tell me what's stopping me,
Cause I won't cry, nope. I can't cry

The moments after,
Sunk by strokes from the keys of an A minor,
Touched
A nerve, with more power in the feeling,
Not the word,
The sharpest curse hasn't been heard,
The dominate curve wasn't reserved,
So I opted to let it burn.
And let the flame reverse.

Why isn't this love working?
Why when I overthink,
It hurts me, times three,
Close the curtains,
Wipe the dust from the shoulder
Owe none to the loaned,
Before you shed, find closure.

Guess whose it is?
You better own it, before she-
Comes, rolling down your cheek,
With a tune so sweet,
Tap that shoulder, no fear,
Flicks on the B chords,
Wipe away the spills,
And the sad part is,
The toughest one dies,
The hardest.
Even harder,
The strongest one, cries for a partner,
and when he's calling,
she's ignoring,

and went it's nothing, it's important,
Why cuddle, if it's cutting, souls?
Why pose for the picture,
Exposing the wrong image,
We go, tired and lonely, down our aisle,
Holding emotions, this here is golden, we can't cry now.

Let Me Explain

You say it's dead and you want to give up,
Grinding gears,
For some years,
You gained attention, from me.

Now, I need to explain,
That I don't want you to leave,
To leave, is leaving the memories,
In my head just to leak.

You keep,
Telling me that it's dead,
Resting in peace,
But that's the piece,
To my heart,
Where light meets dark,
See, if this heart stops beating,
I'd still need that spark.
Don't cut it out,
You better knock it out!

Since the beginning,
All the way til infinity,
Find my feet on the court,
When you're shooting,
The brick is bittersweet.
Baby, try it again,
More than my friend,
Not my enemy,
You get all of this energy.

Don't you keep me wasted!
Why you keep wasting, time.
Saying love is the drug,
That took over your mind.

You say you'll be fine,
Even though you have feelings.

Even though that you know,
I know you cannot forget it.

I know you can forgive him,
Hymns we hummed on rugs,
Silent Night, we cried,
Rapped, then wrapped into hugs.
I know you will think of that,
When the next man does,
Come close to your ear,
Saying you are what he loves…

Saying that he wants to touch,
Your chin, when you grin,
While I touch these thoughts,
With my pen.

I don't really like to sin,
But I was sinning with you.
And now those sins,
Slip away,
And I don't want them too.

You know I want you too, much
That I can't stop.
Walking to pause
The thought just makes my heart drop.

It makes me think deep,
It really makes me sink,
It makes me appreciate - more,
What you're giving me.

Even though it's your fault,
That you don't look like poison,
You look like peace,
When you walk in those Jordan's.

You look like what,
They said I need.

You look like love –songs that I want to sing.

You look like a cookie crumb,
That I want to eat.

I know you're bad,
You are the substance,
And I am the fiend.

Let me expl…

Part Three: A Dash of the Substance

Mama, Please Don't Judge Me

Then there's Maybe...

Maybe Pt. 2

Temptation

Lucille

Oh, Father

Cope

Push that Poison

Part Two

A Walk with Destiny

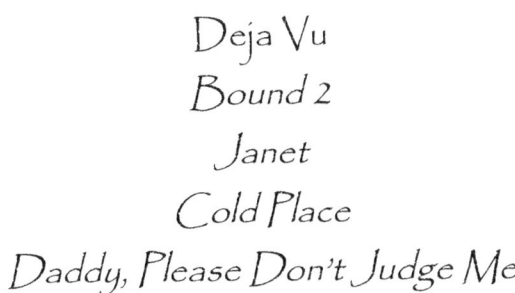

Deja Vu
Bound 2
Janet
Cold Place
Daddy, Please Don't Judge Me

In the Ten Commandments, God tells his children, "Honor your mother and your father, so that it may go well with you and that you may enjoy long life on the earth." This was Gods first commandment with a promise.

When I was younger, each time my mother gave me a whooping, she would say, "I'm only doing this because I love you." For years I wondered what she meant by that when it came from her mouth. Of course, I was young and receiving a whooping or having privileges taken away was how I was disciplined.

I later learned the meaning of my mother's meek but terrifying words. I, just like every other child, had not reached a point in maturity where I would have understood the principles of life. However, they were very simple. Stay out of trouble, stay in a child's place, and stay in line with God.

Even with my rules being that simple, I still broke them, and my parents helped me with suffering the consequences. When God said, "so that *it* may go with you..." He was talking about love. Looking back on when I disobeyed my parents and God, I knew that the punishment I received would only be useful if I decided to grow from it. And as I look at my mistakes and wrong doings, I learn to turn away from them and make better decisions.

The most impactful lesson in life that I learned with that discipline routine, was to listen my mother and father because with their help to teach me to do the right things while I am young, one day I will understand their determination as parents to see me grow into a young man who practices righteous living.

Considering the fact that most of my friends did not live in households under the same home training as I did, I considered this as "love" being passed down to me by my parents. I grew to see the results of a child that grows without the same household training.

Now, I truly understand the meaning behind my mother and father punishing me. It was done out of love and because they wanted to teach me to be the best that I could be in the eyes of God. I am blessed to have the parents that I have. They raised me to be aware of my decisions and always reminded me that no matter how much I would try to hide the truth, it will always come to light in due time. My mother taught her children this lesson at a very young age.

A little bit more about my mother. She always taught me to fear her and respect her. I only feared my mother as a sign of respect. It wasn't that I was scared of her; I was more afraid to lose her love. She reminded me to never put my hands on her or any other woman. She broke lessons down to me like this, "If you look at me with an evil eye, you will look at another woman with an evil eye." Basically what that meant to me was, if I had enough anger inside of me to think evil thoughts towards my mother, who is my foundation of care, it would be nothing for me to do that towards another woman.

When I was 7, she sat me down one day and said, "There's no other woman that's going to love you the way that your mama loves you." Since then, I never questioned my mother's love for me. And last but definitely not least, "Never burn your bridges with your mother. Once you lose your bridges that have been built, it can take a lifetime for them to rebuild." Do yourself a favor and always seek the good in your mother. No matter how difficult your relationship may be. For the love that she has for you, is unconditional and may it cover your soul until the day that you leave the earth she birthed you into.

It was a bit of a task when it came to my parents teaching me about romance and love. That's a lesson they lacked skills in teaching. In my neighborhood, there was never a need for them to teach me about the Birds and the Bees. Being around some of my outside family, having seen new babies added to the family each year, at an early age, through movies and ear hustling, I pretty much put the pieces together.

My mother always taught me about love that comes from God. She would turn the television set off, open up the Holy Bible, and read stories to me and my brothers, sometimes even cousins, about how God controlled the way that love was distributed through people back in the Bible days. I can remember all the way back to the age of five my mother teaching me about God's love. She would always tell me that there is no other love that is greater than God's.

My father on the other hand, taught me about love, between man and woman much more than my mother attempted. You see, my father was never shy when it came to teaching me these lessons. He was the first adult to ever talk to me about sex. I believe I was six years old when we had our first conversation on the subject. He was driving me to school one day and there was a lady who had waved at him as he stopped at a stop sign. We both could tell that this lady was on drugs. She was half dressed and smoking a cigarette walking a child to school. My father looked at me and said, "Don't you be looking at no old woman like that. I don't ever want to see you having no kind of business with no lady like her." I just stared at him and tried to understand what he meant. I thought for a long time before I nervously asked him, "Why?" He said with a disgusted face, "That's a dirty woman. You want you a clean woman."

At the time, I didn't know what he meant exactly by "dirty", but he either meant dirty as in sexually dirty or dirty as a reference to the drugs in her system. Whichever he had meant, it eventually led to him telling me that it's always important to take showers when sleeping with a woman. "If she's dirty and you sleep with her then you'll be dirty too." I understood exactly what he meant when he said that.

On that morning, I learned what HIV/AIDS was. I didn't know the science behind everything, but back when I was six, that's how my father broke it down to me.

Ever since then, I've always looked at women and wondered, "Is she clean or dirty?" I believe that my father was just teaching me to have standards. They say that as a man, your woman should be a reflection of who you are. So, I observe every woman that comes my way to have good judgement about which young or old woman I let get close to me. This message from him carries on in my heart because I feel that when searching for love in someone, you should always have an idea of the type of person that you would enjoy being with.

The older I got, the more I grew from what my father told me. And in some instances, the further I tried to run from what my mother had taught me. I felt like I had to make mistakes so that I can grow from my mistakes. But the truth is, I didn't. I always knew the right choices to make when it came to getting involved with a female, I just felt that making a small wrong decision wouldn't hurt me if I was going to be willing to grow from it. And that was me listening to that *other* voice in my head. Listening to that voice is what took me under.

During my process of learning what love is, I made tons of wrong decisions, and still do. What I, and most people never want to understand, is that love comes with a cost. It offers us a price that we all have to pay in our own different way. The cost is how we are affected by it mentally, physically, emotionally, and spiritually. We all suffer from love in Magic Land.

Our greatest accomplishment in life should be to find God's love by reading His word and making connections with him. God's love holds no suffering. The love in Magic Land is a love grown from mankind. Mankind will leave you looking like a fool the way it makes you suffer. Once we do that, (find God's love) we can find love within ourselves. And once that is fulfilled, we can find love within others. Until we learn to walk down that road and experience that journey, we will continue to live in Magic Land, the land of all fantasy and sin.

Once upon a time, my mother was addicted to crack rocks. You know, drop it in a pipe, light it, smoke it, and get lit? Yeah, those crack rocks. When my mother was on the streets doing drugs, I mostly lived with my uncle and all of his six daughters. While he would work in the day, my grandmother would watch my cousins, brother, and I. In a two-bedroom apartment, with a total of 12 mouths to feed, sometimes, times got rough quick once my brother and I had basically moved in.

I remember always being clueless of why cocaine was such a powerful drug. I would question life and even myself. I didn't understand the value of my own worth, and sometimes I would even start to believe something was wrong with me. I didn't know why crack cocaine made my mother do such stupid things.

During the ages of six, seven and eight, I can remember my mother's life on drugs vividly. Sometimes, she would leave the house for days. I would call her phone, and if she had enough strength to answer a phone call, she would only say "I'll be back home soon baby. Mommy doesn't feel good. When I get better, I'll come back home, okay?" As a six-, seven-, and eight-year-old child, I didn't have much of a choice to believe her or not to. Whenever she did come back, she never seemed to be okay. Her eyes would be as big as an owls. Her skin would look very dark and moist almost as if she just had ran and mile and needed to cool down. She would always have a cigarette with her, and Lord knows, I always hated the smell of cigarettes. We would all be in the living room gathered as a family when she came back to visit. It was sort of like a meeting for everyone in the family. I mean everyone in the family was there to see my mother. That's how long she had been away from us. I could always tell when she was on drugs and when she wasn't. On this day in particular, I believe she was coming down from her high when she came to see us.

She began to tell us all of her stories about how depressed she was and why she felt that her using drugs was helping her. I would sit in her lap and listen. She would say things like,

"It just feels so good, but it hurts so badly. I don't want to leave my kids here. I don't want to be out there smelling funky, getting high, not having my priorities straight. My son is calling me every day and I can't answer the phone because I'm too high to function and I..."

The room would be so quiet. There would at least be twenty people in that small living room in the two-bedroom apartment. At least twenty! When it was someone's chance to speak, everyone spoke and everyone would listen. My uncles and aunts would yell, cry, and yell more. I remember always staring at my grandmother when my mother would be talking.

Sometimes, my grandmother would let me sit near her side on her couch and listen to my mother because she knew that my mother would leave again. My grandmother couldn't speak too loud so we all had to be very quiet when she would say things to my mom. I remember, she said, "You need to get off them drugs and come back home." And that's all she could say before she hung her head down and started to cry.

In the midst of all of this sadness, there was a love that still filled that apartment. Even though my mother would end up kissing me goodbye with alcohol and cigarette scents on her breath, I still felt her love. I knew she loved me, and I knew that she didn't want to leave me. But when she listened to that *other* little voice in her head that told her to keep using her substance as a remedy to heal her; she forgot what it felt like to find remedies within herself without using crack cocaine. That voice would speak to her and say,

"It's okay. Just one more hit. It won't do nothing to you. I'm your friend. C'mon, just light me. You know you want me. You know you want that rush again. Come get it. I'm right here. Right here at the bottom of the pipe. You know where to find me. Smoke me! Terrance will be fine. Your babies will be fine. Besides, they can't help you like I can help you. C'mon. Light me up. That's right. There you go. Yeah!"

That was the devil sweet talking my mother. He was distracting her, making everything that was bad sound so good, and my mother fell for his tricks. The longer that she stayed away from God, was the more she listened to that voice. I'm sure she heard God speaking to her saying,

"What are you doing Christa? You know you have a family at home. All this money you're spending. You know that rent needs to be paid. What about that job I blessed you with? You're not thinking Christa. I won't force you to listen to my voice. Go ahead and live that life full of destruction. I will never let go of you. But you must learn the hard way. Open up my word. (Holy Bible) You know where to find me. Speak to me and listen to my commands. When you decide to come back into my life, I will bless you in my time and give you the desires of your heart."

When I was eight years old, my mother checked into a rehabilitation center and things started to pick back up from there. Without my father or my brother, it was a draining obstacle for her to get back into starting her new life. She had no other option but to put God first and find out who she was in life. Once she started practicing building a strong relationship with God, her life became so much more peaceful. I'm not saying she never felt pain again and everything was perfect, because nobody has a life like that. Nobody ever will. I'm saying that, when she listened to God's voice and put her faith and trust in God, that's when real changes started to come into her life.

During this time of her life, she was teaching me the importance of prayer and building my relationship with God. Before I start to speak on the peace, I have to take you through the time of my life where there was mostly nothing but pain.

This chapter is dedicated to my parents, for I am thankful for everything they have taught me about love. I drift off and capture the stories of lost souls wandering around in Magic Land hurt.

These are stories that cover a period of time in my sophomore year of high school. I was searching to find inspiration in everyone around me. In this particular time, I found all of my inspiration in the negative things life had to offer. I witnessed that poison was affecting my peers just as much as it was affecting me.

Every day I focused on people's moods and faces. I tried to scope people who were hiding their pain. I learned that you notice so much more in life when you are quiet and observant. A quiet soul equals a learning body. When I found motivation within myself, I would spark a conversation with some of my peers and ask them their perspectives on the dark side of love. Here are some of the stories that I wrote while using their voice as my inspiration to write about the poison that we all are victim to living in.

Mama, Please Don't Judge Me

Mama, please tell me, is this all ironic?
"There won't be rainy days like this no more"
That, you promised
Well there's a storm now; Hearts are torn now
And I'm just being honest,
I'm hurt,
And my soul is getting soggy in the dirt.
Please, don't judge me

I've been playing too hard lately
Falling off the monkey bars
Swinging so life can break me
There's no grass stains on my jeans yet
Though my genes have been worn down
From generations
Somehow, I still feel the arranged,
When I kiss her after she said she doesn't feel the same
It's a shame
My shoes are soaked - due to the rain
I should be inside,
Though it feels like home is where I'm all alone
Away from comfort zones
Home never really feels like home
I'm trynna cope,
Hoping that the rope ties around my throat,
Cause the poison has a price,
And I'm broke.

Mama, please don't judge me
Cause I like to wash the knifes
When I do dishes
Mama, do you get the picture?
Love, is but a fright
On the pages under water
Thought I found it,
But the only thing I found, was
That I'm drowning

In Magic Land
And I don't know how to get out; there are no maps here
You said,
"There won't be rainy days like this"
But maybe there will
Maybe they will...

Then there's Maybe

Maybe it's cause…
I was into Leo's, and I didn't think for the opposite
Cranberry shot of lust which was very provocative
Which led my lips under…
Way under, just a stray lover

May stubborn be inflictive upon pride?
May pride be inflictive with different horoscopes?
The more I grow; I feel, I'm just way too emotional

But I'm a Cancer
So, just forget it…

And fall victim to "love" almighty
Or lust, if you look hard enough,

You'll find me

I just might be under, way under
Bound to fall and wander after I wonder

Maybe it's cause…
Love isn't vivid, No pun intended, and when I had it
Yes I admit it, I refused to kiss it
Only because I've witnessed so many innocent souls visit
Moments, where bad wishes come from a mistress
French kissing good stories goodbye for dirty business
Wishing it didn't happen,
You wish you weren't attracted,
You're wishing for this disaster, to die.

Maybe it's cause…
The feelings inside, won't start needing "love"
Until the world start feeding "lust" into the minds
See, that's exactly why I'm stuck,
Paralyzed, and out of luck
Terrorized and trying to…
Before the time ticks out

Don't let those cold stones grow in ya' mouth

Down south where she blew like winds,
Winter was at its bitter end
Maybe she was into two types of guys, like Gemini's
Or Pisces?
Virgos, vanish after lashing at breakfast,
I passed and passed out.

Forget about mourning,
I proposed the toast and swallowed the poison.
I asked her

"Where are we going?"

She said, "Nowhere important."

I said, "Where is that?"

She said, "Nowhere."

And kept on pouring.

Maybe Pt. 2

When the voice in your head tells you, "Don't go. Please, don't go!" Turning away from that voice can be the first step you take that leads a strong mind towards sin.

Life is mostly mental. The strongest people are those who connect with themselves mentally. When your inner voice tells you, "Don't go" and you listen to it, that's a sign that you are aware of God working within you.

When you hear that voice saying "Don't go" and you do go, you are then turning away from God. And also turning away from yourself. Don't become comfortable with turning away from yourself. The more that you turn away from yourself, the more that you get lost. Distractions only lead to more distractions. Distractions destroy and dominate your true character.

How do I get better at knowing which voice is which?

Pray to God for knowledge of self and the will and desire to stay focused on your journey. A key to living a life with less stress and more happiness starts with knowledge of self. Knowing who you are gives you the ability to make better judgement of things. If you don't know who you are, you think according to what everyone and anything else leads you to think.

To inherit happiness, you must know what you enjoy. To inherit love, you must know who you are. To even give love, you must know who you are. As you grow, you will hear and feel convicted by one voice when you turn away from it. One voice can make you feel very guilty and ashamed of yourself. The other, will send joy and happiness into your life when you listen to it and make good decisions.

The "Know Yourself" procedure takes a person years to understand. Every day there are many choices the human mind has to make. You have the power to exercise your mind and change the ways that you think. When you learn to know yourself, you learn which voice to listen to. Practice listening to the voice that leads you down the right path in life. For this can be a babystep into finding true love and happiness in your life.

And maybe,
If we just started falling for our types,
Than being tied,
Before the battlefield of life.

We could be all that we can be,
And learn to appreciate everything.
But since we're just pretending,
That we know what love means,
We will be here for a while,
And you know what that means.

We're just going to be stuck here.

Temptation

I'm getting weak,
I told you I wouldn't do this,
I told you girl,
I can't really handle my daddy's music,
He was just into it,
Intuitive and elusive,
He had me listen to Pac,
But Pac wasn't confusing.

It wasn't until,
He switched to Al Green,
And Smokey Rob,
That my problems,
Jumped on my back,
Cruising, then I was lost.

I told you I wouldn't do this,
Do those things with the cool kids,
Cool off, and somehow,
Feel I'm the coolest.

How did you do it, daddy?
Sadly, I am clueless,
The bass hit,
And that's when I saw you complacent,
Until somebody started complaining.

I told you I wouldn't do this,
Now I feel like feeling life,
I feel I'm moving,
Slower than I ought to,
I hope it doesn't cost you,
A dollar, like it did for Kendrick,
Predicament swerve.

I told you I wouldn't do this,
And I'm killing the vibe.
I know that I'm just a student,

No more questions alright?

I'm tested with temptation,
I'm tempted to flee,
I'm telling you,
Take those telling eyes off of me.
I am weak, right now.

Lucille

Please come back where you belong...

Indian silk scarf to shield her edges
Grasping the section wherever her body held the lemons
Or lime
Strawberry or maybe even
Vickie's secret in the evening

> *Or hollow stories in the morning*
> *Still mourning for a meaning.*

Her skills so proficient
She's a pro, need I mention
Her tongue rolls for the business
Forgive her

Her mama is a doctor

> *Yeah, they all watch her*

Blow kisses to her audience
Imagine all the positives,
Her daughter grips the unexpected curse
Sneaking 2 by 2's in her purse
It's funny how quick,
She gets a bitter soul to vison,
The back side of her front
Without a glimpse of her pu-

See, she could make you think that you want her,
Pops studied Psychology in his younger days.
It's funny...
Cause she's the only woman that learned to take his money-
And abuse him for his love, for fun.

Ha, but I can't even laugh, because
It started in Jacuzzi baths with scented suds
At sunset, I looked in her eyes, realizing
I sunk

She never took my cash.
But in the end - she had - the very last laugh.
Lucille, Lucille,
Please come back where you belong.
Even if I hate your guts; Even if you're wrong,
I can't resist the skill that you picked up from your mom,
So sing me a little song,
Like Richie.

Oh, Father

Oh, Father,
God I've been missing you,
Missing all your calls,
Oh, father, I am just a sinner who.

Fails in his lesson,
Praying for peace and progression,
Handling pieces of art,
As a shield of protection.

I'm a victim,
Only because sins make me feel like I'm winning,
I'm just spinning,
Spending quality time,
With the appealing,
Substance, my parents loved it,
They say it did them some healing-

Oh, Father,
Is it true – is it true?
Is this the love - you commanded I not go to?

Well, I'm present,
And my present is being presented,
The perks on perspectives,
Of a living legend,
Living life reckless.

I keep my eyes open.
Wide open for the occasion,
And close them wire shut when I'm praying.

Truth in your own efforts stick to you more.
You can't take what other people say and do and assume that their learning
will stick to you. You have to learn for yourself. You cannot watch a person
eat and expect for you to get a full stomach. We are victims because we
want to be victims. We love being victimized. Shall we change that Oh
Father?

Yes, my son. Yes, you all shall.

Cope

How does a man cope?
While he thinks of using ropes to end misery?

How does a woman cope?
When she loves shoving things down her throat,
To wash away her pain?

How does a teen cope?
Daps and pounds to all of those who did them wrong
Waving what's up, but never in touch, communicating?
Even when they say,
"I know, how you feel"
They don't.

And for the girl with a broken heart,
How does she cope?
How does she ever - turn to the word hope?
When every time she used it
He smashed it and abused it?
If you picked her heart,
Would you still want to hold it?

Her booty was big - but her heart was bigger,
Knowing that,
Would you drop it down or would you heal her?

I know that she knows the answer
So we both figured
The issue.

I forgive you – if you don't know how to answer,
How does the boy with a solid heart cope?
After he, depends on pills to travel down his throat,
After he, rolls the weed and inhales the smoke
After he, boils crumbs on top of stove pots,
Oops - I forgot,
He doesn't.

So guess who - he turns to?
The pretty girl with a broken heart covered in perfume,
That makes him feel like loving,
Is the last thing to cover, his feelings-
She cares for his healing,
Only after the fact.

After he crashed,
After he passes,
After you laughed at how miserable,
He was, you love, how unpredictable,
The dimmed lights get - when the vision goes bad,
How do you expect for him to cope with that?

How do you cope?
Hope do you know,
They aren't lying when they say they love you?

Is the honesty behind you?
Does the honesty hold you?
Right near the angels,
But you would still question surveillance,
From lovers who master the art?

Scared that love will hurt you
Sooner or later - burn you
Bring out the worst,
Just letting it burn,
Is worse - than acting like doesn't,
Even if love wasn't
Something worth touching.
Would you stick your hand in the cookie jar
And get busted?

I know,
You'll feel empty,
And the feelings inferior
Make you feel you can't cope

Even if you held onto hope,

You wouldn't know
How it feels to be filled with love and enrichment
Fulfilling the space with dents dead in the middle
Eyes wide open while you swallow the thrill.
Head on the pillow; thoughts in the gutter
Under covers sinking,
Dreaming of that someone,
To be there to comfort – you,
Dreaming of a lover who-
Isn't even there.

Push that Poison

Isn't it a pain to see a beautiful girl in so much?
Cry for help, all torn up, is her heart
And she handles tons of emotions backhanding her face
Poison all in her cup and placed across her plate

A redbone girl with a smile isn't poison
She strikes with concordance – she's independent.
All she wants is for you to stop pretending,
As if you care, and actually pray for her, like you say

I know this young girl and she's about 17
With 7 screams and hectic dreams as she cries herself to sleep
A razor blade isn't safe for play – she cuts away her wounds
But a shade of grey love…
Holds her smile so one day she can bloom

She stares out of a window and she sees a red moon
Stooping and waiting for revelation to resume
Her end is far more wishing than a pair of new shoes
So I grab her by the hand and make her laugh
On most occasions
I say something wrong and water will start racing
Down to the floor from her eyelids
Covering her face just to cry a bit
Ashamed of her creation
I hate how she's so tied within
Herself

So I blame it on the young guys
Who know this young girl?
The ones who never let her vent and get it out
Rather than helping her express - they push more in
So baby has to learn to push that poison.

Loving all the noises that she can make
Ignoring all the pain - he creates

Baby, push that poison

Isn't it a pain to see such a beautiful girl in so much?
Cry for help

Part Two

But you see there's this guy that I'm close to
And I don't think I'm supposed to
Share this, but I will
Just to help
You

Just another young man, strung over the low ends
With no father to guide him,
Just a stressed mother beside him
Two older brothers on the other end of his eyelids
And their actions replace his father's duties doing backflips

Back to the story, there's that young girl
Loaded with excitement to rumble his rough world
She's nice and nasty but I'll keep the private quiet

It wasn't until she fell in love with quick feet for lust
Until he learned to put her in the proper position - to make her thrust
For satisfaction, pleasure, and a bit more satisfaction
Leading to sadder reactions on a Saturday morning when she passed
it

Passed the news by his ear just to drop off the message,
To keep or not to keep was a difficult question,
What to do, two hearts headed in the wrong direction,
And both minds are bumping to grind
A smooth hard headed child

She cries

Wishing that she never opened her legs up
And he is now in the same situation his dad was
She looks around in corners steady searching for cameras
There's no evidence it's his, he's still searching for answers
The tension is hitting harder than hammers
17, but in reality, they just soaked their pajamas

If you know what I'm trynna get after

Now both, afraid of the future, thoughts rest on the same platter
After the sex, there's confusion
And confusion is damage
And the drive for sex that they both had, no longer is massive
No laughs in aisle 6 - where the pampers sit

She sits

Worrying about how her mother will handle it
Aside his heart,
He's burning cause,
He knows his mom can't handle it
And in their minds they carry candles prepared to ignite the kid
Before he breathes
Before he laughs
Before he grows to see all of the beautiful things.

It's Poison

Should've thought of that while sucking her persuasion making noises
Now everything can be slimmed down into one word
Pointless,
Cause she's wet at the eye and no longer needs his ointment
When she was wet at the time
She didn't seek the importance
Of protection.
So, as tears race down her face
She's stuck in relief from depression.
The baby races and beats both of its parents
To heaven

Because she-
Couldn't handle-
The poison.

A Walk with Destiny

Kinds of cute
When she struts with plastic nines at her hip
With bred 11's on her feet
And lips that push away to receive
Lust printed on every cheek that she had visits with

The type of girl to wear booty shorts in the winter
Tank tops in December
So that all the boys would remember
Her body,
Like Eve to Adams eye
The type of girl to make the guys sin
Before they get a chance to try
If it's worth it

All she ever talked about was...
All she ever wanted was some...
All she needed was some...
Soul, to show her what a real man is like
How it feels to be princess, or a queen
To wear a diamond ring
To scream of satisfaction without pain going deep
Into the center.

Sinner, things got hard,
She showered in his laughter
Instead of showering under covers with pain pushing faster
Not at birth - but after
Her daddy said

I brought you in this world,
Let me take you out
Gladly

5-star dinners
Just to make her feel happy

Til' he got her in a room at night
And dimmed the lights
Sadly

Now isn't that worth care?

Poor little Destiny won't even shed tears
She just struts in the summertime switching all that...
While the boys look at Destiny calling dips and grabs,

"Girl, you nasty"

Now isn't that worth confusion?
What would you say - if I said - she was a straight A student?
What would you say if I told you she had full blown aids?
So she shows her body expressing she needs to be praised?
A sex slave,
Because her father touched her whole frame
So she struts with redemption to secretly erase the pain
Afraid, to love any man that comes her way.

Her purity completely damaged
In the past completely vanished
She doesn't know how to say it
Because her father never practiced
With the care to teach her how to keep a balance
The young boys love to take advantage
Poison, she sips it,
Refusing, and they take it as a challenge
They abuse her,
But still she - tells herself she's beautiful

Poor little Destiny
Lost inside of her flesh

Taking away your breaths
As it melts
As it burns
Would you focus on her heart?
Or be distracted by her curves?
Would you love her in the dark?
Where nobody can see?
Would you bow on your knees?
And surprise her with a ring?
Or would you look through her heart,
Deny her pain and avoid it?
I bet you wouldn't dare to
Take a sip of her
Poison

Déjà Vu

I got you
Even when he makes you cry
When he lies to cover fabricated vacations
When I see it all written in colors of neon depicted
When you're in my presence,
You're slowing becoming the opposite of his fiction
And I know it

It's been quiet without his stick shift driving you
Cause lately I've been peeking out of my window spying you
Creeping on the side so that I'll plant my "I" in you
So that I can too,
Be the one that you turn to,
At two o'clock in the morning
When those tears are steady pouring
And you're sinking how I sunk

I swear I found perfection in your atrium
As well as, the way you tilt your head as you laugh
I become vibrantly numb
All in reference of imagination

I've been drinking your tears for a minute
I know the taste
You cry, I sip, and you don't want to complain
You know that I'm the one for those lips
Knowing that I fit the curve on your hips
When they pressed against my pelvis
We melted
And you know it
But you rather cry and act like there's no way that you can show it
We stand against the rights
But it feels so wrong
Am I right?

"Everything is alright.
Girl, I got you"

And if no one else is down to catch when you fall
Then, guess who…
Teenage Documentaries
Filmed all from my perspective
Are the only things left to mirror what's inferior?
Open up

You're so mother-loving serious

One in a million and the story is still similar
Could've been, should've been,
But I never spit a bitter word
To your face, though you spit the sweetest ones on my tongue
I'd savor, to let them burn and melt
Never felt the nerve to confess to you how I felt
Because when laughing your head would slowly tilt
And I could see the truth resting on your pupils, beautiful.

I only held back so you could finish the race
I started but can't finish
Cause it's built up so much ache
Reminds me of the November every time I awake
See your face and know that you're soon be drifting away
Just like everything amazing
Once golden, but now it's fading away
And I see the changes

You flicked my soul to create a spark
On every single thought

I only wanted to steal your heart, temporarily.

So that I could pick it up and place it at the top
With the angels by my side so that it would never drop
Like I said

"I got you"

Even when water drips from my eyelids
To kiss my nostrils
I want you to show me how to bleed
Every time I think of distance
Every time I glance at the pictures and look at the description
Of him

Will you ever think about that?
I got you, and you got me, but I see you choose to go back
You got me tightly wrapped in my wishes
"You got me" but I'm throwing knifes staring in the mirror
Throwing pots cause of temper
Heating spoons in the kitchen
Of my heart

It's time to come out and do the dishes
Cause this home isn't a home,
And my throne is no longer worthy
Started as friends and grew as homies
Man!

It's lovely rather funny
And so funny how it's nothing
But it's something
'Cause you love me
Well,
At least that's what you tell me
At least that's what you told me
But I never let it help me
I just wanted what I never had
And you had it
Had you not
I'd never master thoughts of smoothly taking
You
Out on dates in restaurants
To carry on
The right love vibes that feel wrong
Am I wrong?

For loving someone
Someone who I trust?
Someone who can blow all negatives away in one
Tote
Placed you at the top of loves totem pole
And you've grown looking down
While I've been taking shots spilling out

A chemist at the heart
Though we're not really into science
Illuminating another's essence dipped in loyal vibrancies
I've made you shine before the light
Dwelled within my eyes
Now I'm dwelling
Therefore, My cup
Runneth over
I need you
To add a little dash of clear closure
The exposure of my love
Isn't done spilling out for you
I'll be spilling steady sipping
Reminiscing Déjà vu

Until it all comes back to me
I'll be tragically
Injecting the lethal
Until I see you.

Bound 2

I left my soul back home in the closet
Even left mama's prayer request to sleep in my wallet
Left misery in the back of the doctor's office
I fist fought my profit
I've picked up some knowledge
And on the journey I have found
Several ways to drown
Bound
To fall in love

I overcame agony
Due to depression
In the depths of alleyways
I've crept like Billie Jean's victim
Never shook hands with my mistress
I held the handle to my teacups with pride
Blind in the mirror
Cutting my soul deep with precision
Scissors and a vision couldn't make a vivid picture
So I cropped out every smile
Though that wasn't my intention

I've been missing
I've been hiding with Mr. Hendrix
While Mary blows him kisses
And he kisses the sky,
I search for remedies and they seem harder to find
Cause Jimi stole them all
So I fall
Even harder

Bound to fall
In love with drugs
Depart from trust
And double lust
Because
I don't know
Who brought me here?
Therefore, I fear

Who I am today
Slip, slide, and fade away
Bound to
Fall
In Love.

Janet

Is it wrong for me to ask you if you've ever made love?

Have you ever raped lust in the kitchen?
While thunder trembles above your head?
Can you overpower the rain without permission?
Have you ever caught yourself crying in the mirror?
Poetic, cutting the pain so you can feel different?
I know it hurts to stay away from loves intervention
I know - that you - don't know - the difference
Between love and lust
Janet, oh Janet.

I thought you would've peeped
Peeking into your soul so long until it screamed
Speaking into wholes for so long until you made one
Never felt that you could create your misery by mistake, huh?

We believed that love was for those who fell already
Girl, I'm falling.
Eyes blind open,
I focus just to hear your heart calling
At an-an-an-anytime,
You'll be different if I'm missing you,
Investing time to spend with you.
So I daze before your pupils,
So I'll find just what you want
Not me, but remedies that'll lead you
Inside of me, squeeze, breathe…
I believe, you – came.
For justice.

Janet, have you ever made love?
Come quick,
Pecking hot words while tongue kissing your trust
There's more than thunder and rain
Calling our names
At any time you can get it
If you're searching for pleasure

But whatever,
Love is back in the woods,
We in the desert.

Oh, Janet
You never had it like this, have you?
Let the bass bumps grow to confuse you
You're not losing
You're a winner
You're just choosing to lose
Lucy is sitting in your mirror,
While you sit there confused,
Oh Janet.

Did Michael teach you all of those moves?
You can move me,
Like planets moving after the moon,
You are a movie.
You're satisfaction - morning cartoon
You're the sweetest.

And then she bounced into another cocoon.
She was dreaming,
And I was finally having fun.

Cold Place

This isn't my canvas,
And I've been running for a minute,
I got the hint,
This right here is no palace.

I'm in a cold place,
I'm near a proper approach,
And a "No thanks"
Between the platinum and gold,
I'll pick a ruby,
The color of Rosie,
Colors my soul.

I need some heat in this cold place,
I need balance,
I need prayer and time to rest,
I need a challenge.

You keep on asking,
Is it a rock or hard places?
If it's a mansion,
You can't help me pull the plug to save it,
So let's just face it-

I'm at an all-time low, love.
I know you lost your mom,
She's lost hitting those stones, love.
Is what she's searching for,
She's hurting more,
For her fix.
I know you're mad,
So find your balance in the midst of this.

Life is ridiculous,
But beautiful, when I look at you,
Beautiful,
To the fullest,
And frankly,

I'm just an introvert,
X'ing all of your worries.

I just focus on you,
For clarity because I'm hurting,
You are my vivid,
In other words – life isn't so blurry – with you.

Daddy, Please Don't Judge Me

But I guess I can't complain,
I'm the lonely wrong victim
I'm a mistress, I'm used to it
I admit it
I'm addicted
To the Poison
That you bring
Not complaining
Still sippin'
Finding empathy
Through 2-day-old bottles of Hennessy

I know you taught me to treat these ladies like queens
Treat them like diamonds
So that diamonds would never scream
Their value
I hope, I didn't learn to doubt you
I'm just bad news
Written in the famous paper

I savor every moment that's golden
What's cherished is unspoken of nowadays
Now, I praise
Whatever doesn't make me feel ugly,
Please,
Daddy, please don't judge me

I've learned to not listen
I'm not too hard headed
I just ignore good intentions
I want to live my own life and grow old not pretending,
I love every breath inhaled
I still forgot to mention
I want love...
Sleeping in the basement,
Can we die after hugs?
I want to know that I'm loved - daily

I want long kisses
Warm hugs and conversation.
Maybe that will make me,
Maybe,
I don't need another... maybe...
Daddy please, don't.

Part Four: A Jungle in Kalifornia

The Jungle
High off Lust
If Love Never Existed
Sweet Dreams
Snakes in the Garden
Purple Pigeons
Beauty and the Beast
Park Bench
Neptune's Daughter

Remember that Sasha is rather than a true character in the story, but "she" is a living metaphor. Sasha represents the female side of love. Throughout the story she is used to embody and present the perspective of a young woman who is searching to find love.

This chapter was written to combine both The Good Kid and Sasha's minds together to better explain the image of what it feels like to be in Magic Land. "A Jungle in California" represents the crazy life's that the both of them lived growing up in California. While Sasha still has her dreams and nightmares; The Good Kid tries to explain what he sees as he is living and taking a journey through Magic Land by himself. He is no longer with Sasha, but her perspective in Magic Land still is brought to his attention. He is still lost wandering around trying to find himself.

Together, they are, mentally, not physically. Here are the stories of two young souls on a journey to find what love truly is.

The Jungle

Welcome to the Jungle
Where hearts get crushed and seem invisible
The jungle where "somebody" turns into "nobody"
And everyone close runs away
Uncles and aunties told you to pray
When you're too close to a victim
And there's not too much to say
They're fake.

Players play in the night; learning comes in the day
If heads are right, I guess it's the quiet ones who escape
So what are you?

This is where fantasies come daily
Where the lions and saber-toothed tigers are meditating
The jungle where they sit and spray
Cupid's arrow
Every other day than Valentines'
Handle my – lovely daze.

You'll run miles and miles
To never reach a destination
Just roaming and creating
More pain in bloodstreams
Where you can feel your heart scream,
While dreaming...

The jungle where demons hop on your back
They whisper
Throwing you off track, remember
This is land of no emotion
If it's growing; kill it.
The higher you are,
The harder you fall
The harder it hits when you; feel it.

No maps, No understanding, No patience
Just time, space, and more time
They said it never rains in Magic Land
But, I guess it will tonight,
Stay tuned

High off Lust

I've been drankin'

Cranberry shots of lust
In zones where reality power hugs emotions
And the path of normality closes
Closest to my skull
Did you ever feel that we could be so dull?
So full of sadness
Because happiness was limited right after we crashed

We woke up in confusion, outro's, interludes,
Then we ran it back round'

Until we covered imperfections underground
The pressure bursting pipes - in my life - made us smile

Lord, forgive me
Kissing the sky with tears shed because she's so pretty
Lord, forgive me
I woke up in confusion, when the sky started to kiss me
Meaning her baby blue eyes
Do you get me?

Back then, I dreamed of superheroes
Coming to my rescue
And you were strong,
So, you know?
My superhero was you

We flew into the limelight and circled with the owls
Never thought that you'd pick me up just to drop me back down
We woke up in confusion

Outro's,
Interludes,
Then we'd run it back around.
And around, and around, and around, we would go
Because of our disparity we walked miles, until hope
Got the best of us.

We created love times lust by two in a bundle,
And we never figured out how
We would ever escape
From this jungle.

If Love Never Existed

Would we still hold optimistic
Visions of change
Or would we all play the game
Correctly

If love never existed
My tears would fall from waterfalls
Instead of times temptation called
And wrapped me smoothly in her palms

If love never existed
My mother would've never had me
Your mother would've never had you
But that's half true

What is love anyway?
Something you do
Something you feel
When you look in the mirror
Around your face, or just a phase?

If love wasn't present
What would we be sexing for?
Honeymoons?
The moments of pleasure is what we call love
Right after the pain, we go on searching for lust
Nuts to bust
And they look at us, wrong for being honest

Hmm, isn't that the problem?
Hiding the meaning in the meetings creating odd ones
Someway we found pleasure through beautiful letters
Lessons, sex, actions, proving that you love her
Do you love her?

Or is it only when it spills like butter?
Under the covers tented over gardens
After slipping into her under garments

Utilizing noises just to block out all the problems
"Making love"
Passing through uncontrollable stages
Is how you satisfy and write your story on the pages?
That's how you prove what love is even when you lost the cadence?
No.

Balance, "Wait for love, its magic."
Acknowledge, love was never in you
Until they peeled you open.
Worried on the way back, they laughed, as you were floating.

Unleashed, they all turned away from your care
So you can grow to be loving

Is love still in the air?

If love never existed
Who in Magic Land would care?
The perfect example? Or the lovers still near?

Why would you fear to be heartbroken?
If love wasn't a token to happiness
Would you be the happiest?
Or notice something's wrong?

If you said yes, then you are wrong
Cause if love never existed,
You'd be happy in your home.
You wouldn't search to find love
If it never belonged, here.
Who in the world, told you that it belonged here?

Where is love?
Can you see it?
Can you feel it?
Is it present; is it spilling?
Is it poison?
An addiction to a sober soul living
With issues, on the outskirts, it seems so appealing
Why do they define it as something so healing?

It was here.
During the day of the beginning
Adam and Eve
Couldn't even fight the feeling
Would it even matter if love never existed?
Would you still be that soul crying in the mirror?
Love is from the heart
Love is just a vision
If we took it out tonight,
Tomorrow, how will life be different?

Sweet Dreams

Sweet Dreams stuck in a jungle
Rumbles and night
Cuddled with hearts that've been crumbled
Tumbling on a crisscrossed pathway
Until the wrath waves
Collapse safe
When my eyes are closed
Sweet Dreams

Tell me what you know about dreams
You don't really know about nightmares
Despite the lime nightlife that rides near
To remind fear to attack

Boogie monsters in the dark breathing on your neck
Tell me what you know about less-
Stress for the mind
Stimulated so that you can carry on
They hit love bongs and blew the O's in your peripheral
Vision is limited
When the greatest gift is gone

Peace
Tell me what you know about beetles and snakes
Untamed in the garden when broken hearts harden
Tell me what you know about dreams
Cause I haven't been to sleep in a couple days
And I haven't loved with separation from my battle cage
So

I don't whether I should sink or float
                              In this jungle...
Night and day, today, tonight
At night I seem to fumble
Did I stutter pushing out those crumbled words?

                                        I-I-I love you?

Tell me what you know about lullabies
Rested behind my eyelids revealing lies
Twisted and opposite of everything that became
Sweet dreams in the jungle never rested if he sang...

Snakes in the Garden

Just like the serpent of Eden
Snakes slither their tongue
For only one reason
To strike poison in those believing, it's lies

Only if Eve wasn't so beautiful
Adam would've still been plucking on the peaches
But Eve had the audacity to offer a tasty treat
He never knew that a simple bite could lead…
This far
He would've never stared so hard letting coaxing defeat
The purpose
That is, only if Eve wasn't so beautiful
While pressed below his neck slightly sliding her nail cuticles
Singing. Oh, she was singing.

Intentions of a serpent with intentions to contradict you
How could that be?
Rattling in shaky moments,
Plotting on how he'll kiss you.
You'd say anything to excuse the absence of etiquette as he tricks
you
Quick to loan you quickies
Repairing your emptiness to make you feel that he can "fix you"

Scratching you in the grass, he holds your aspects,
while your abs rest on the tip of hell's volcano
The magic that's been too cool for your clues to bloom, erupts
There you lay down toasted in blood covered in lust.
Good luck!
Escaping from the garden.
Where pythons want to kiss you and show you a little something.
Cuddling in your presence to three-ever keep you smiling,
Slithering down humping your mind on your neck like medallions

This is the garden where the snakes,
Love getting a little taste then forsake for the basics.

This is home for broken hearts dripping under the pavement, still dreaming.
Tongue kissing cobras with immaculate features.
This is - the moment when the ventricles start leaking out
Emotions start screaming out

Thank you Adam,
I appreciate it Eve.
Sincerely,
The rose that sings while his heart bleed.

Purple Pigeons

Pure ripper roles
Eyes seek it all upside down
Whatever is backwards is attached
Mixtapes looped from love scratches
High off the high cracked vinyl's

"Don't you break that needle baby"

Eyes can breathe it upside down
If needed, baby.

Slow it down
Cause those needles...
Yeah, I need those

What type of lovers play with pigeons?
What type of lovers mix red roses and blue violets
To create a purple vision?
Hurdling through imagination
Lost but dedicated
To the cost that leaves a heart bankrupt
Pecking poisonous grapes and pushing past perfect raisins
Just to be dried out

Don't knock it
You forgot that
Pigeons are far distant from profits

Licking the blood off the leaves
Until they stop sick
Nonsense in the middle of the street
Jaywalking with intentions of getting caught with hummingbirds and
blue jays
As rebels, they can sing their pain away
Purple

Blue days and black evenings
Lions intrigued by bubbly melodies
Blinded by simplicity in being rebellious
But they're all just invisibly jealous
By pride.
Smile, if purple pigeons dance before your eyes.

Pure ripper roles

Eyes seek it all upside down
Whatever is backwards is attached
Mixtapes looped from love scratches
High off the high cracked vinyls

"Don't break that needle baby.
Cause those needles...
Yeah, I need those."

Beauty and the Beast

I used to care about popular people,
Popping all of my problems with heathens,
Catching a cold barely breathing,
I used to give my secrets,
I used to,
Do all the little things I wasn't used to.

Used to, boasting on beats,
When I explode,
Closing, two minds,
Two lives, for fun, running with three…
Foreplay laced for one reason,

"What's that son?"
"Uhhhhh. Pops, you know…I need love."

Beauty, truly in a bottle.
She sits there,
Immortally important
We can push back time behind sources
You've been moaning for extortion
I've been growing into a portion
Of everything I isn't,
Improper, but you get it.
From time, comes experience
From that, grows difference
I'm different from ignorant.

But you,
You're a beast.
With a crown over your peeled back eyebrows on fleek.
Don't speak,
You know I know the secrets.
You used to tell me everything,
Everything fell to pieces.
All of you was peace,
Plus a little bit of demon,
Don't we get a little sneaky?

When guardians are upstairs sleeping?

Anyway, you get the point.
I sneak dissed honesty,
Until the rust,
Began to rush on our hands from our promise rings.

Park Bench

Baby girl sitting on the park bench,
Shoes off,
She was looking lost,
Exhausted.

Probably tired of the traffic scene,
Probably tired of her boyfriend,
All those fantasies…

She's probably tired of her family.
Probably tired,
Of being tired.
I heard that line so many times,
It should be retired.

In the woodchips,
I watched her move,
To the swings,
Monkey bars,
And through the tube,
She started sliding down the slide,
She didn't use her smile,
I guess the ups from childhood days,
Have been gone for a while.
It took a while.

For me to stop and ask her for her name,
I thought of proper,
Introduction, I sensed the pain,
I look her in the face,
Saying, "How do you do?"
She say, "I don't do much. Ha, ha, what do you do?
I said, "I do, like you…"
(Awkward stare)

And then I took it back,
She said, "Oh really? Tell me what you do?
I said, "I lack –

In conversations, I don't really talk to strangers,
I stay away from dangers - but today,
I found a light in you."

She smiled to only say, "Really? Yo! That's kind've cool. I like that
fire dude, I walk around searching to fine my life by finding you.
Well I mean, people - *like* you. People who seem to care. I listen to
music that takes me on a flight of stairs. And oh, I really love nappy
my hair. Don't be afraid to stare. Is that enough for you?

I parked my bottom on the bench,
And then opened my mind.
She started singing sweet,

> *Ain't no sunshine – when she's gone,* (Doom doom doomp)
> *It's not warm when she's away…* (Doom doom doomp)
> *Ain't no sunshine when she's gone,*
> *And she's always gone too long,*
> *Anytime, she goes away…* (Deem doom doomp)

I tried to smile at her,
But then I shed a tear,
She say, "Why do you cry butterfly, sunshine is here"
She pointed at my heart,
And I pointed at hers,
I said, "I know sunshine is bright - but why it gotta burn?
Why do I gotta hurt? Why do we gotta grief?
We are we sitting on this park bench getting deep?"
She said, "Something told you put your foot close to me,
From a distance -
You knew that you weren't supposed to be,
Dreaming of me,
Dreaming of me - hurting,
Pretending you were okay,
Checking if I was hurting.

You say you - deserve this,
But this is what has come.
You say you're never happy,
And you want to - find love.

But if you find love,
What you gonna do with me?
That baby boy is you,
This is love,
And I am,
She.

Go ahead and clear you're throat...
Here's another rose...
Give to receive...
And watch the lovers grow..."

Neptune's Daughter

Since I've known her,
We've both been yearning,
We've both been hurting,
Turning our shoulders to the wrong people.

We've sinned a couple of sins,
But I never labeled it evil,
We bounced around jackpots,
Creating a love casino.

She blossomed we know,
She traveled through zones,
If poison came tagging along,
She would find her way home.

But she always kept running back.
She could see how I'd react,
She could see my hands – sweaty,
She would give me little daps.

She would give me long hugs,
One with the universe,
She went to Neptune,
And came back with a verse,
Tattooed on her tongue,
She refused to live and hum,
She decided giving hugs,
Was easier than giving up.

She sang sweet songs, to me.
All night long.
She was a product of a profit,
Who is an idol?

She was a queen,
Now her spirit, is free.
And, she used to cry,
Now she smiles if she speaks.

She won't speak too much,
She is one with the moon.
She sleeps in the woods,
And leaves them too soon.

She says she's okay,
I try to believe.
But if I'm not okay,
Then why would she leave?

She won't answer the phone,
If I call her today.
But if she did,
This I surely think, she would say.

"I've been there before. I've found a new vibe. A natural vibe. I feel so alive. I know how it feels; but I am done with that pain. I loved and I loved, and I'm done with her games. I've seen the lights shine bright on me. I've been low; Remember when you couldn't help me? I remember being lost. I remember being cold. I remember, the little advice that you told. I remember you would tell me that you were a rose. A rose that dreamed to walk the broken road. Young rose, you promised to help me grow.

And now that I've grown, you keep calling my phone. Why you calling my phone? Why can't you let me go? I'm that product of a profit, who is an idol. I am living today, I am living so free. I found a new love. Don't you handcuff me! Don't you steal my freedom! Don't you take my shine! Don't you give me that look! Don't you kill my vibe! Don't you love me, T? Don't you do, like you say? Why you look so confused? Why you looking away? T, Please don't do this! T, Please don't cry! T, wipe those tears. It will be alright. You'll be fine T, remember? It felt so right? I told you it was wrong. Now look at our lives. I'm sorry T! I'm sorry! Don't call me again, let go of my hand. I'm sorry T, so sorry.

We were everything once; now we can't be friends. I'm sorry T! I'm sorry. Now you're looking at me different, so I'm running to religion. I've been swimming in this poison. Now, I'm running into distance. All of our dreams are twisted. Redemption isn't practiced, love is no longer vivid. This wasn't the picture we pictured when we took pictures. I'm leaving to live, and living to leave every intention, with you."

Part Five: Nightmares on L Street

Lost
Too Faithfoul
Fire Red Tea
Eve, Oh, Spirits
A Million
Trust Issues
9094
Sumchin' For the Mind
Voodoo Child Blues
Time's A Wastin'

The Right Night
They Say
Look, Learn and Listen
Rich in Spirit
Imagine
Nightmare on L Street

Half way through my high school journey, I started to witness different forms of love. I started to understand more of how life really was. Life was no longer a Disney movie for me. I started to realize that people lie. Family lies. Friends lie. Girlfriends lie to your boys. Your boys lie to their girlfriends. Teachers lie to students. The government lies to the world. But most importantly, I learned that we lie to ourselves. I started to imagine my life as one long path –something like a forever going 100-meter dash and that's when I started to take life for what it was.

I had plenty of friends who I would hang with daily. At lunch and after school friends and I would mess around freestyle rapping about lifestyles we never had, cars we never drove, and guns we never held. To me it seemed as if we were all story tellers. We all had stories to tell. I was just the only one who picked up my pen and wrote my stories down.

At home, life was much muted for me. I never really enjoyed being at home because it seemed as even though I had a loving family with food and shelter, I was still learning the ways of life on my own. I never told my parents that, but that's why I would always come home late. I wasn't out selling drugs, or even doing drugs. I wasn't out partying or having sex. Most of the time, I'd walk around campus talking to myself and meditating. You can ask anyone who knew me from freshman year to junior year, that's all I ever did. It was just me and my headphones.

And once my phone died it was straight meditation. I didn't really talk much outside of class. I was more into focusing on those freestyles, like I said, "the things I didn't have." All the time that I spent on separating myself from people, I was learning. I was taking the pieces that life gave me that I didn't understand, and overtime I puzzled them.

I remember the day I told my friends that I was going to write a book about my life. My best friend, Dajah Williams, and I were talking about how one day I would be famous for being a storyteller. I kid you not, ever since I met that girl, I swear, she's been my motivation. She was one of the girls in my life who would take these walks with me at lunch. And we would circle around campus and talk about the way life changes and how things for the both of us were moving so fast.

Most of the stories in this chapter in a serious way were all driven by the conversations we had. She would explain her thoughts to me about love and lust so well, that it was almost like she was taking everything in my mind, and just saying it in her own words. I could finish most of her sentences because I knew exactly what she was going through. It wasn't until I met Dajah, that I really began to carefully analyze the differences between love and lust.

Unfortunately, she ended moving back to her home back in Cleveland, Ohio. She is definitely, still to this day, my best friend and still teaches me the ups and down of this game called love. In a way, it feels as if she was teaching me everything that I needed to know. Man, do I miss her. We were both going through the same issues in our lives and if it wasn't for her, the whole idea of L Street would have probably never come about. This one's for you pro.

I know you are wondering where in the world is L Street and what significant meaning it has that ties into this story. Let's just say the "L" stands for "Lust, Love, & Loyalty" all in one. According to Dictionary.com, a *nightmare* is a bad dream that brings out strong feelings of fear, terror, distress, or anxiety. In this case, these "Nightmares on L Street" derive from expectations gone wrong in relationships.

Whether it be a high school relationship or a 20-year strong marriage. One thing that I have learned through observation is that in relationships, expectations are invisibly stationary. One lover may have an expectation on the other and when those expectations are not met let me tell you, things can get ill. I've seen it happen. I remember as a kid, my father would expect my mother to do certain things and as soon as she let him down, everything between them, for only a certain amount of time, would go downhill. And vice versa.

I've also witnessed this with my aunts and uncles. My cousins and I would go spend a night at my aunt's house when we were younger. Every time expectations went wrong, we could feel the tension between my aunts and uncles grow thick. They would start arguing and fussing and all of my cousins would giggle and look right past it. The thing that killed me as a child was watching them pretend as if everything was all good.

They would keep composure and act as if inside they weren't burning in anger. Looking back at it, I understand why they would act "okay" in front of us. They knew we were watching and knew how to act when we were watching. This taught me so much about love in a marriage.

From my uncle, I learned that sometimes, you have to let the woman win. As a man, you have to be the bigger person. From my aunty, I learned that a woman has to be strong and stand firm on having courage and self-respect.

At the same time, from her, I learned that as a woman, it is not easy to be strong. It is something that takes years of practice of patience. After they would finish arguing, I would be the one who sat there and stared at my aunty to see if she was going to start crying again or not. When my uncle would storm off and everyone hopped on the game; I hopped into my aunts arms. On Earth, there is no love without pain. This was just one of those things that I could see early on.

In my own household, my mother and father had their very own ups and downs until November 30, 2004, the day my father passed away. Before that time, they always found their ways back to the same bedroom resting together. Through that I could easily see that love was not perfect like the peaches. What I mean by that is, with a lifetime bond, there will be obstacles that both lovers will have to overcome in order to stay together.

Once I saw that imagine, that was how I viewed relationships in my youth. Though I wasn't writing books about how I felt at the time, it was instilled in me that love is visible. Love is something that you see. So many people say that you can't *see* love. Wrong. I could see it perfectly. I saw when love was high. I felt it in the air when my father would play R. Kelly in the living room and grab my mother by her waist and step in the name of love with her. My brother and I would peek from upstairs past our bedtime quietly watching them dance, hug, kiss, and sing the night away in joy.

There was also the times when I saw the lows of love. Such as, when my mother had tears in her eyes and a desire for what the world had to offer. One night, she had enough of the arguing and she left. I remember I was six years old, laying on my father's chest at night watching *Law & Order*, and I asked him, "Where's mom? When is she coming back? Can you call her one more time?" I wish I remembered the words he told me that night, but I don't. I do remember the look in his eyes though.

More importantly, I remember the tension in his body that became stronger every time I asked a question. He tried so hard to hold it all in. He tried so hard to not tell me what really went down, why my mother wasn't in her bed at night and when she was coming back home. I will always remember this night. I feel asleep next to my father and that's all I can remember.

At six years old, that was my lesson learned. In relationships, nothing is perfect. I don't care if it's Jay Z and Beyoncé. No two lovers on this earth are perfect. I could definitely see when love was functioning in my family just by expectations alone. At the end of every night, my uncles and aunts would also go right back to one another. After everything that killed them mentally; they still stayed together. That's love. There was almost no way to heal these broken promises but through time and forgiveness.

It was harder to see it clear. We are now like a bowl of cereal, one rusted spoon, and a cold gallon of rotten milk. In other words, I guess we just have to do what we have to do. Better put some water on those Cheerios like Grandma Christine used to. Maybe we can even pour some red Gatorade in the bowl. Not used to it huh? Neither am I. But sometimes, I guess you just have to do what you have to do.

My grandma used to always look me in the eye and cringe her face and feed me a strange emotion. I was not mature enough to know why she stared; rather than spoke. There were certain ways that she would fix her face to look at me. Those faces of hers would tell me everything that I needed to comprehend.

Grandma Christine would sit on the living room couch and daily watch the news. Actually, it was *Jerry Springer* or *Maury* more than the news, which just showed her "I'm too old for this, someone entertain me" personality. I'd be right next to her on the floor watching as well and I'd glance at her. She'd stare at the television as if she didn't see me and she would say to reassure me, "I'm looking right at you, boy." And there she would go, cringing and grinning at me.

Grandma Christine went to her house in heaven in 2010. I can only remember so much about her, but what I do remember, helped me get to this story.

We, are now like a bowl of cereal with rotten milk still in the gallon. Like, a custom made airplane, with flat tires for landing. Meaning whenever we crash, oh baby, we're crashing. Whenever we remember how it feels to fall, we do anything it takes to stay in the air. We are a backpack with broken zippers. We are a dozen of musty and dead flowers. A lollipop with no flavor. A kiss with no meaning. A sad song, with no feelings to spare. Two butterflies in a box. Two souls with....

Two souls with two souls. If that makes sense. Two souls that can only be pleased by lust and money, so if we do not own any cents, then we don't add up. Nothing ever made much sense to me since all my loved ones passed away. I was young. Very young. I guess I just had to find a sensation to stimulate my five senses.

I see why Grandma Christine always ate her cereal with water in it. She was teaching us a lesson. She was teaching us how to love life for what it is. What man makes for good is not always good. She would eat Cheerios with water instead of milk and claim that the water was healthier for her system. While everyone was disgusted by her theory, it actually made much sense. In a way, Grandma Christine teaches us that love has its own taste. "Don't let nobody tell you how to love life, or anything in life. Love is what you make it to be. The same way water and cereal heals me, when I replace milk, is the same way that yourself and live shall combine, to define what love is."

Life is what you make it, and so is love. No matter what you hear, it is up to you to decide what you want to believe. You have to taste life, and see what taste good to you and what does not. Those little things that you may come across while living that make your soul fuzz, brighten your day, and inspire you to spread love, are worth holding onto. Anything that touches your soul and has that unexplainable vibe, is love.

Cherish those moments life gives you every chance you can. And share those moments with others. Just how Grandma Christine's love is forever remembered, by the serious conversations as well as the loose and goofy ones, people will pass on your stories. They will remember you for the love that you shared. They will forever love you, for they love that you shared with the world. Plant this garden with ice cold water.

Lost

Loving the thought of last time,
How in the world do birds wipe their tears?
If all the bull is for the birds,
Are they winded?
Pressing every button.

Push,
Until the bears, chimps, and skunks,
Make love in the damn,
How do we become one near the lamps?

What's the price Mr. Ape?
What can I do here-
For my soul not to taint?
For these lows to escape?

Got crabs climbing trees,
Giraffes near the leaves,
Sharks in the shade, near the shady old souls,
Snakes, in the place, where the grass never grows,
Venom in the soil,
Pain under my toes,
Evil in the winds,
Wicked people win,
Atmosphere,
Whispering, "Don't you let them in"

This right here is wow,
This right here shows why my mind is shut down,
This here, teaches why I'll never turn around.
They say, you're slowly rising,
Then they say you're slowly dying.
Then the birds sing songs,

And I reply, "Yeah, I'm trying."

Where are the eyes to witness?
The birds wiping their tears as they drip?

How in the world do birds wipe those tears?
I'm so lost.
Aren't you too?
Cover my eyes,
Don't get lost,
The solution, is rooted in you.

Too FaithFoul

That's when my heart starts racing,
And my stomach starts aching,
Tripping over shoelaces,
Holding faith in two phases,
Two faces,
Too famous, of a story,
See the face of Alori,
When strings lace all around my face,
Two stories,
Building,
She sits on top of the building,
Fulfilling her dreams,
No longer scared of the man,
That's awake when she sleeps.

There he go,
Creeping round' the corner,
Too faithfoul,
Now he's crossing at the border,
Torturing her heart with a torch,
Back tracking,
To smile when she looks back in intercourse.

Of course,
That's when my hands start shaking,
And my promise is sacred,
And I watch his wife bathe naked,
There I go,
Doing things like David,
There he go,
Undressed, hiding in the basement.

Impatient,
But enough rhythm to keep the cadence,
He lost his steps,
Lip gloss and skin marks all across his chest,
His woman never wished for a calm confession,
She learned her lesson,

Now, she second guesses the messages that were sent from her best friend.

There she go,
Heaven sent a smile so lovely,
A smile like honey,
A smile switching only at one speed.

"Touch me." She whispered "What's with the distance?"
"Friends don't kiss."
"I won't stop you. But listen here, this is addiction."
"If you're with it, I'm with it."
"You just don't get it."
"Hold up boo. This isn't you!"
"This can't be true."
"Wait, I'm confused."
"Don't be. I know you feel lonely. I know the wrong can feel so right sometimes low-key. I'm waiting for you to show me."
"Hush those lips… hold me."
"I'll hold you. There's just some things I need for you to show me. Take off your clothes slowly. And maybe we can…"

Go deep.
Deeper and deeper I go,
There she go,
Creeping back, I guess that's good for my ego.
As long as he won't,
Call, asking for her when she's here with me,
I hope she doesn't call asking whose house is he…
All of sudden, loving is redundant,
As for me, my heart beats faster,
We both watch the phone ring.

"Hello?"
"Yeah, Yo! It's me"
"Yo!"
"I think, I just saw A kissing on B"
"What? In the parking lot? In his back seat?"
"Don't worry G, I'll be there soon."

"Get off of me"
She starts to scream,
One strike, her lip starts to bleed,
She swings back, his eye gushed,
Nobody's looking up,
One look, was just another problem B.
Out the back seat,
He walked out, bound for apologies,
I shouldn't have,
I shouldn't have,
I shouldn't have chea-
Bow! His knees hit the center of L Street.

Man, that's when my hands started shaking.

Fire Red Tea

First they hate you,
Then they love you,
Then they hate you all over again.

She pointed to the grey clouds,
And started shrugging.
She knew none from the present,
When she presented, she loved it.
She stuck close to her good side,
Flipping through scraps,
Dipping the dots, and flicking the dabs,
Swallowing tea.

It ran like Olympic,
Picture the liquid behind her pigment,
In love with,
The things we viewed as disgusting.

Moonwalks over thorn bushes,
Picking her roses,
Sunflowers kissed the tip of her nose,
When she closed-
Her eyes, she was raped by the stones,
She heard Roman cry,
Like a dungeon dragon.

She pointed to the water,
To put her foot in,
Wouldn't it be best if I couldn't?
The rest of her days were worse memories,
Never did she see,
Love on Sunday mornings.

She pointed at the demons like she was cool with them,
With one chance, she bounced back into ooh sipping,
Two pinned to the tulips,
Too frigid, of a lady,
Criss crossed on the two-steps,

Am I cool yet?

You bet,
The light shattered,
Her mind gathered, what she was missing.
Loving the broken visions,
Fire red.

Eve, Oh Spirits

I hope you didn't forget why,
I hope your head remembers,
I hope you know,
Nightmares arrive the most in December
Stay silent.

Love smelled like flowers,
Every hour,
I continued writing.

I hope you know Santa isn't...
Mindful of our silence,
Divide these gifts
And little boys and girls are not reminded,
To value little things,
Eve, oh.

She can't see through the weed smoke,
The gas, gassing her up,
We die, as little people,
Beat by beat, heart to heart,
Left right left, we all fall down.

I'm cutting my conscience searching for closure,
Can't find
Closure in the land of magic,
Voodoo is how we decline,
Rewind, to when grandma taught us the meaning of love
Rewind, to when two cousins would fight and make up,
Rewind, to when mom and dad weren't arguing cause,
They'd rewind, missing the present,
Forget a present,
We're stuck, in the same box.

Eve oh,
I know you don't want to remember,
These nightmares arrive the most in the month of December.
These nightlights have no juice,
And the bed keeps shaking
She held her face,
As she heard a voice,
Saying **BE brave**

A Million

I don't really know what it is,
I've just been falling and failing.
Inhaling, exhaling, and selling-myself.

I've been listening to Vandross,
He says a million's not too much,
Kisses from you,
Fractured my walk since we grew up.

I don't know what to call this,
I don't who is calling,
Dry leaves with blood to fall,
I feel the callings' cough with caution

I just continue walking.
I'm afraid of the moments,
I was once hemophobic,
Opting to kill optimistic visions

I'm living, baby.
There's one way to the top,
I'm on my mission, baby.
Don't you ever tell me to stop.
I got a vision, baby.
I'm a sinner, I don't listen,
But please forgive me, baby.
I'll make a difference,
I can't hope for meals with millions, baby.
I sin, only to win,
Don't follow my entrance,
One day I'll be where I wish

You would thank me,
Just thank me, later.
You can take me,
Places, I pray that you just cater, to my needs.

You plant the seed,

That grew into a man like me,
And from my rib,
I gave to you,
I know I'm missing some things.

You'll be by my side.

Trust Issues

I started peeping the open secrets
Men lie and women lie,
Trust sits before the deepest love.

Once lies are compulsive and habitual,
Connections split in two,
And trust bonds slip on slopes
Feelings go down the drain,
Memories will fade away,
Everything tomorrow won't matter,
Everything yesterday,
Will be forgotten.

It's like the vibes rotten,
It's like the switch up was a stick up,
Which was common.

We used to trust another,
We had the strongest link,
Now every time we sit inside,
We can't even speak,
I say "I'm good"
"No, you're not good"
And that's what makes me scream.

Sometimes I think you think,
That it's not good to think,
About what you think about,
Before thinking to speak.

I bet I make you think,
And maybe you should think?
Next time,
Before choosing to lie to me?
Maybe?

Think about it.
I never used to doubt it.

And if I did - I didn't have to question,
My faith was in your words,
My worries never rested,
On my conscious forever.

I never knew what it meant to not be able to put your trust in someone. I always thought you could trust someone even if they lied to you a million times. I see it like this, trusting someone is a choice. Everyone has that choice to believe or not believe. Once I started to tell myself, "Nope. That doesn't sound right. Find the truth in that for once. Stop being scared. The truth will set you free, go find it."

I understood that trust is far more than just believing in someone or something. It's more than a decision also. Trust can be broken down to the root of why we stand on certain things. We trust in the chair to hold us up before we sit down in it. We trust in the bed to not break when we decide to sleep on it. We even trust in the shower water to stay the same temperature and not burn us while we bathe.

Trust, is sometimes considered the root of why we do what we do. Look at what happened from me trusting you. How could I ever truly trust anyone else after being lied to? Would you still drive the car if you knew the brakes were broken? Would you still sleep in the jungle knowing that bears, snakes, and lions are present during the night? Why trust in something that gives you the bad vibe by just thinking of it. I promise, you will never catch me sleeping in any jungle with lions near. That's me just making good judgement of what may happen. Why would I continue to trust when I know what is bound to happen when choosing to trust in one who lies?

Don't believe everything that you "hear."
Don't believe everything that you "see."
Until you see everything.
Feel me?

9094

There were nine of us,
Plus the parents.
Sunflower seeds in plastic cups,
Plus a gold necklace,
Sleeping in alcohol,
The floor had nine pillows,
The night had nine widows,
Roaches on my window,
Racing behind the curtains,
We were so little.
Behind those blinds,
My young eyes were blind,
To the sad riddles.

Paint on the wall, still chipping.
Stains on the rug,
Please forgive me,
I laughed.
He was in the bathroom sadly coughing up blood,
When done,
Stormed to the bedroom - receiving the love.

Outside life – wasn't quite right.
What up blood, what's up cuz'?
Handshake, hit the bud,
Laugh hard, when it hurts,
Give a hug, that was love,
In my eyes.

Why was I having nightmares?
I never understood why life
Offered me nightmares.

I took a trip to Caminito Mindy,
And the winds were windy,
I was humbled; I was numb,
And I was feeling empty.

JC had been crushed,
So I was crushed too.
Expression of lost kid,
All I can do is love you.

You make me go back in my mind,
And want to hug you,
I wish I would've told you I loved you,
That day.
I wish I would've never let you,
Leave my way.
Since then,
Nothing has ever been the same,
I went to 9094,
And felt you in my veins.

I don't write these words in vain,
I'm just writing out my pain,
And emotion,
I miss you,
And I've really been growing.

Without you.

Sumchin' for the mind

Life is like an everlasting merry go round.
We conquer and we fail,
We search to find and sometimes we don't find,
Anything.

We look back and realize,
We finally understand.
We move forward,
Then, search for pillows.

We rest.
Some choose to push harder than others,
Some choose to not do much.
Some are gone too fast,
Some stay too long.
Some do not pay attention to time.

Some worship ideal gods, certain lifestyles, materialistic treasures,
natural things, the birds and the bees, the winds and the seas, the him
and the she.

Life is like an everlasting merry go round.
Some hop through different towns,
Some smile and some frown,
Some fail to find importance in traveling,
Some do not care about what is happening,
Millions of miles away from planet Earth,
And that hurts someone.

A man just hurt someone,
And a young girl just made someone smile,
Someone just stubbed there toe on their mothers bed,
Someone is hiding.

Someone may be fighting,
Someone may be crying,
Someone may be dying,
Someone may be flying,

Someone may be shying,
Away from someone.

Something may be driving, someone.
To be a better someone.
Let this little life drive you.

Nightmares aren't always bad. I always used my nightmares and converted them into lessons. Once, when I was asleep, I dreamt of being interrupted from my dream around 4:00 a.m. This night, I was sleeping on my back for some reason. All I can remember is someone walking very slowly towards me. I couldn't see their face, but as I was dreaming this, I remember thinking of who it was. I was trying to puzzle the pieces together. He crept closer and I stared harder. He reached his hand to land right before my nose and then paused. I stared at his fingerprints.

For some reason they were visible to me even though the room filled with darkness. I remained calm. Next thing I know, he came closer and I began to get up. He grabbed the back of my neck with one hand and covered my mouth with the next. I was breathing calm and never said a word. This man caused me no harm while holding me in his hands. I believed he was trying to heal me or teach me something. It felt like I was in a Kung Fu flick and a Kung Fu master guy was coming to heal me while I was resting. I started to wonder "What's next man, dang. C'mon where's the good stuff?" but nothing happened. Right when the "I', in my dream, decided to go back to sleep, that's when the man caused me harm. His hands started to press against my nose and mouth harder. I was defenseless and 100% not prepared for that attack.

I remember closing my eyes and opening them every couple of seconds, fighting for my life with swings and kicks. But no matter what I did, every second I was being suffocated. Of course, I was dreaming. If I truly wanted to defeat this man, I could've simply dreamed it. I let him suffocate me. I gave him the perfect opportunity to do anything he wanted to do to me.

In certain stages of sleep, humans have the power to control their dreams. I believe the reason that I didn't stop the man from touching my face was because during that time of my life I was practicing to expect good from all types of people. I was not scared at all. I believed that nothing could hurt me. And once I put that trust in mankind, the man in my dream tried to kill me.

Rather than this scaring me, I woke up from my dream smiling. Some would call that a nightmare. I call it a lesson. Nightmares sometimes appear to be episodes of what you are most afraid of or what you meant for good coming back to haunt you.

How do you put love and nightmares into the same sentence? Well, that's pretty simple. Some say that love is something you feel. Others say love is something that you do. And there is a portion of people who say love is a twisted combination of both. Love has expectations. Believe it or not, we all put an expectation on love. You expect love to feel some way or for someone to do certain things to prove their love to you.

With that being said, without expression and emotion there isn't much to clarify what love truly is. Same as nightmares. Who is to say what a nightmare truly is, when my nightmare to me wasn't a nightmare? I had my own perspective on it, and turned it into a lesson. I gave my nightmare a title. What does this have to do with trust issues? Well, when you put your trust into the wrong people and the wrong things, that choice can come back and haunt you. It can come back and hurt you also. Be careful with who you trust. If you are looking for someone to trust, my advice is trust God and learn to trust your gut.

Voodoo Child Blues

Before I turn around,
Let me turn it down,
Feel a little tingle at the edge of my hand.

In the middle of mountains,
Windmills and dry winds,
Guitar flicks and 5 spills,
Baby, slow down.

The edge of my hand,
Wiping the sweat,
Let me tell the secret,
Once I had me a woman,
She didn't keep it.

Freedom won't pay the bills.
I never meant to hurt,
You never meant to, either,
Least' that's what we heard.

Can I get a window seat?
Without a whisper testing me?
I just want your lips to meet,
Lipton tea,
Sweet temptation.

Baby, I got the blues,
And I'm down to lose,
You, just to find myself.
So give me the clues.

I ask for help,
True, but that never helps.
And yes I know you try,
But trying never felt,
What it feels to die,
Where the love is dry,
Where high fives and sundresses don't satisfy.

So please, give me room.
Kiss my dignity,
And my identity,
So much it forms a river sweet.

I get the blues, wondering if you gon' remember me.

Time's A Wastin'

I've been drifting,
93 on the 94 W,
Loving you, too hard.

Too much, fussing and fighting,
Not enough living and vibing.
Not enough flipping excitement,
But a butt,
Shivers in silence.
Time's a wastin.

Who was searching for perfect?
Who was looking at me?
Who promised you the apple?
Would fall far from her tree?

Who would drown in the droops?
Who still handles the fruit?
Who will catch me when I'm happy?
As I'm falling for you?

I enjoy being a raisin,
While you are the grape.

Assuring to you that,
Love is printed before your face.

You whispered - you need a soldier,
I need a soulmate.

You are my T,
And all the truth in love we can surely taste.

Times a wastin'
Spend it on a vacation, faithfully.
We can travel into intimacy,
Escape with me.

Sometimes we don't want to live.
Sometimes, I have to take,
Just to be able to give.
Sometimes I get emotional,
And can't control sins,
So I slow time down,
So us both, can live.

The Right Night

And if I die before I wake,
Nobody can hold me,
More than I can hold myself.

Nobody can help me,
Even if I helped myself,
I'd be hurting,
They say God's just working, mysteriously.

Sometimes,
I say that he just loves to disagree,
Ever since I've been loving,
Love is no longer giving me,
What I've been asking for.

But tonight is the right night,
And if I die before I wake,
Don't eject my night light.
I've been loving.
And you've been loving,

                                  Out of my eyesight.
Snap back to reality,
Rearrange your timeline.
Until time is back with me.

Last night, I had a dream,
Dreaming of tight rides,
Tight hugs, tight love,
Tying lies, in my life,
Tired of tanning my tactics,
Trying to tamper the task,
Taking hands off my dreads,
Symbolizing the head.

Memorizing pieces,
Speechless, but you comprehend.
That you killed me,

When you decided to sleep in my bed.

Though this is figure of speech,
Your tease killed the fin,
So the fish no longer swims,
In the sea, he can't see.

You're the two headed shark,
I'm the shrimp, so let's eat?
Don't you see – that
You were always stronger than me?

So I left, but you kept coming - back for me.
Until one day,
I ran out of food to feed.

You were very hungry,
And hunger means somebody bleeds.
Meaning, it's meaningful,
To swallow pride every time we meet

So as I sit here dreaming,
About a story to write.
I swim into a dream,
Which was a story of mine.
A story that explains - how you came in my life,
To eat,
And not worry about my appetite.

This is my nightmare,
I was starving to death.
Your promises were my goodies;
They vanished when you left.

See, I don't want to eat,
With you anymore.
I'm just the fish that lost a fin,
Now, I'm flopping at shore.

I was once right there,

I was losing my life.
Then the water touched my gills,
And I opened my eyes.

So baby,
If I die - before I wake.
I promise I will never eat from the same plate,
As you, I look at you, and go…

Should've listened to mama,
She told me so…

Oh she told me.

They Say...

They say, that they'll
Be there for me.

Apparently,
I'm too good at acting fine,
Or I just need some therapy.

I don't want no therapy,
Talking is a mental thing,
I'd rather sing to birds,
Than girls, acting like they care for me.

They say,
I'll make it far.

Sad to say, baby, I've been braking hard,
And brakes aren't too good on this car.

I'm rolling downhill.
I made it - very far,
But I enjoy the thrill.
You know this drive can kill.

Nobody's driving safe,
I looked at that text that you texted me,
Responding late.

Where you at, love?
Does it matter, T?

Oops wrong number,
That was family.
She wasn't mad at me,
But she peeped game.
She dug inside her heart
Expressing how the love changed.

She played the same game,
And we dribbled some,
Back then,

211

I remember, it was really fun.
But now we're separate,
And very desperate,
To find something,
That we know we'll never get.

They say,
It lasts,
A lifetime.

And maybe,
Til infinity.

But if it ever,
Dies out,
They all start remembering.

That expectations are crazy,
She gets caught with her baby,
He gets lost in the maybe,
Maybe,
They moved too fast

Maybe,
A little whisper,
While driving,
Can make you crash.

Pay attention to that,
Don't be,
Like me.

Look, Learn and Listen

Don't listen to the slang,
Don't listen to accents,
Or the language of dialogues,
Listen to a little thing called emotion.

Listen with your eyes,
But as well – with your heart.

I bet you're listing,
Things in your head,
I know that you're listening,
To the voice in your head,
As well as mine.

So imagine.

We spend so much time talking,
Listing our thoughts to others,
Speaking out loud,
But how much time do we really spend,
Just listening.

Listen,
Birds,
Planes,
Cars,
Are all things that reassure movement?
Have you been paying attention to them?

Listen,
So that one day you can play with the pigeons,
Moving, just to discover,
Everything you've been missing.

Listen.

Rich in Sprit

Rich in spirit
Poor in health
Broken in emotion
In debt with death,
Dumb with the scantrons,
I was never loved,
For my A's,
Yet affection, was depression skipping sway through my day.

I closed my eyes,
And love was all that I ever gave.
Mind, body, soul,
Trapped in a damped cage.

The more I'm connected,
Is the more that I slip away
It's just funny,
Mama forgot to remind me of these days.

I pray, every night that I get it right.
And if I stop searching,
Love will be in my life.
And if I stop hurting,
My lungs wouldn't be so tight,
When I'm fighting the lows,
The lord knows what he's doing.

I'm still to instill, His word in my mind.
Praise, like I can't praise,
Like a brain and a pipe,
Put together,

I don't want that trip.
My cousins are down,
My uncles gave me the tips.
My mama was hitting it,
Just to feel as one.
Then it punched her in the face,

Let's say, she found love.

And then, love became a different game,
You see that son?
You get caught,
She was catching all her years to come.

So if you're getting B's,
Chirp like birds and eat the seeds,
Believe, you can come close,
If you come clean.
Defeat what it kills,
And build on one thing,
That soft beep,
That speaks to your mind,
When you sleep.

Imagine

Massive crashes clashing after,
These disasters, grasp her faster,
Master, match her,
Have the hazard,
Cross the caution,
Calm me down,
Can you imagine?

A million souls trynna' imagine?
Faster separation,
Clouded segregation,
Vast elimination,
The lemonade of life,
Sweet feet, fear the heavily pebble,
Settle the people,
Screw tests to the neck of the Beatles.
Bobbing the heads, instead of testing dips in the beakers,
Injecting the needles,
Doctor, do we really need those?
Imagine.

If hood doctors, were little homies cousins,
If that was my big brother,
Would he then mean something?
Society, it don't mean nothing,
Sobriety, I won't be puffing,
Conjunction. I run in, million mindsets, why test? Why stress? Let's
learn.

Imagine if Einstein, looked back and chose my pen,
Would he scribble the speed?
Of every second ticking to reach, ways to escape, roots a family tree.
Room for improvement,
Too quick, to bash in breeze.

Things I know, I couldn't tell ya.
If I tell ya, secrets,
Secrets test and arrest,

But are you resting?

Grasp the ventilation - mass hallucinations,
Carrying on the cadence,
Imagine,
If little junior, went to school to be a nudist, move, so he could show
the purity in puberty, passive.

Imagine if,
Yeezus didn't teach us that Jesus still walks, would I talk?
Or the preacher who's raping Keisha,
Be lucky on Sunday's,
While heating the people's heart.

Believing, we can play the part,
Eating off of the masters card - speeding off in the masters car,
She failed to go too far,
Imagine, If Einstein, saw the future - through her walls.

Massive crashes clashing after,
These disasters, grasp her faster,
Master, match her,
Have the hazard,
Cross the caution,
Calm me down,
Can you imagine?

Black & mild - wild cocoons.
Alcoholics, round the room,
Bound to do,
Sins - and,
Lord don't want to forgive them,
Lord, don't give him that scripture,
Imagine, how he tense up,
He cries about the POW,
And tells the fam how much he miss us.
He lie and say yesterday he only forgot to mention.
That he is a sinner like you,
Will you pay him attention?

Imagine, if you did.
Imagine, a million souls trynna' imagine,
Massive reactions running down cheeks of the nation,
How would you face it?
How would you take the stones?
And turn those adjacent?
Those souls,
Can you imagine?
A million faces,
Trynna image?

I imagine that, when I dream.

Nightmare on L Street

As two lovers pop in the twine,
Intertwined and confused.
One feels accomplished,
The other has the blues.

One feels enormous,
The other dormant and true.
Wishing the distant was compact.

Sitting on the edge of the Black River,
She whispered.
                    "Now I'm mad."
And in my head,
We trembled and trembled…

This time we've got ourselves into the dip,
Flipping the subject,
Proving points that never made any sense.
Making dollars,
Spending dollars falling for regrets,
They were pretty in the present tense,
Yes I always said…

This, in many different ways.
This little dream is twisted,
And this sin, we keep sinning,
Doesn't feel any different.

Why you used to this? Why you hurting me?
You take feelings,
But I don't consider it burglary.

I stare, as you sleep,
And the world flows.
And our dreams turn into nightmares,
We do not control.

We had the perfect opportunity,

To up and go,
But the pillow held us down,
Expecting us to grow.

Our dreams are fine windows to the lovely taste,
That we love so much,
We'd rather not be awake.
So when our dream starts to flip into a nightmare,
The caution of being protected,
Loses all care.

"Meaning" fades off,
Cherished memories?
Lose some value,
And can be replaced by anything.

If you start to focus – on something new,
Love can stop in one direction,
Surprising you.

See you can look for love,
In a million places.

But you can't feed a fish food,
If it don't want to take it.

When you are done embracing,
All that the past holds,
You find a new love,
You as a whole, grow.

You as a two, stop.
Two becomes one.
Individually,
One becomes numb.

One becomes what,
One would never think.

One is still in a nightmare,

As the other dreams.

One has been robbed.
One appreciates.
Love is love,
And love can take you to a deep place.

One understands,
Love's not a suite stay,
One is reimbursed,
When one finds that sweet place.

Love is patient with you,
Love is kind too.
But love will leave you,
If you let love pass by you.

Don't love it too much,
Love is a thrill.
Love is emotion,
Love is a hill.

If you get up,
Love is amazing.
But on your way down,
It can get crazy.

I, know you don't,
Want to stop dreaming.
I see you sleep,
And I know you're thinking.
I, see you breathing,
Those precious breaths,
But I caught your murmurs,
And followed your steps,

This surely isn't,
The life that you want.
This, is the lesson,
That grandmamma taught.

This, is the fight, she already fought.

This is a nightmare,
That comes when you sleep.
This is what happens,
When you're loving me.

If I loved you,
I would still stay.
But I started walking,
As meaning decayed.

This - is my weakness,
Keep this discrete.
Have a nice life,

Would you like your receipt?

Part Six: Conversations with the Shaker

Can I Ask You Something? (Sonnet 40)
Around That Time (Sonnet 18)
And Then... (Sonnet 116)
Love is such (Sonnet 105)
Why Fear? (Sonnet 145)
Last Time (Sonnet 152)
The Last Letter, Pal

She said,

"Why were the words broken down like that? Did they really have
significance? Was he just adding some flavor? Was he only
entertaining adults minds in little baby bodies? Was he crazy? Are
his words still amazing? I understand it's creative. Was he just
craving that lady?

Why did he put "thou" in "the's" position? Was The Shaker so wise,
that many years after, he'd know we'd listen? What if his story isn't,
what we think it is? What if his motive is different? What if we look
at what he says but everything is still twisted? What if we look again
and still don't comprehend what the mission is? What if he
mentioned everything he wanted to mention, but burned a million
pages to hide all of his true feelings? What if he had a secret for his
secret? His secret, told me, not to say a thing, and I believe it.

It's like the more that he didn't say, the more praise he gained for
speaking. But what if, all along his heart was leaking, with a poem
to cover the pain, as he kept on breathing, singing symphonies in a
basement, loving the isolation, shoving lines in his face, as a phase,
to face the heartache? What if he was searching, in the very same
way that Sasha did? Would you shake the dust off his books that are
stored in the cabinets? See, that's where I found it. With the lights
off,

What if, I picked up where he left off?

Then a cold whisper scattered,
And she got up and ran after...

Can I Ask You Something? (Sonnet 40)

Excuse me Shaker,
I do not wish to kid.
I do not wish of you,
To fall back - due to offense.

Why did you forgive the robbery thief?
Why did you love being lascivious?
Why did you sip the poison?
If you knew of its bitterness?

Shaker,
That love, your love, that had a true love calling,
Was conformation-
You created because you were falling?

And the blaming was a game,
That she kept on playing,
And you would bear hatred,
Falling down was something you loved hating.

This is the 40,
For your people refusing to know.
Answering love calls,
When it rings after 4.

Casting the love flaws,
So the thieves can flow,
And rob you from that woman,
You forgave her though…

Young shaker,
This is the 40,
Ounce you didn't guzzle.
Down to drown unfitting the unfit puzzle.

The 40th time,
She didn't care for rebuttals,
And didn't care for you,

Slipping through all of her love puddles.

Isn't this the 40th minute after midnight?
After you stormed off,
Telling yourself you'll be alright?

I do not mean to offend.
Shaker,
Can I ask you something?
Love is your drug huh?
And love is corruption.

Love is just an excuse,
That moved you.
Out of the house,
Lust had you knocked out on the couch, huh?

And she,
Pointed the finger and said,
"Get out!" huh?

And you,
Didn't want to accept those truths,
So you,
Keep writing,
While dying to survive,
And she,
Had him right by her side,
And you,
Never learned to accept those truths,
So she poured the poison,
All over you.

And onto your shoes,
You walked and slipped,
And guzzled the 40,
That had you bent,
And she strolled off,
And he just smirked,
And you just stood there looking hurt.

Young Shaker,

I do not mean to offend.
But she stole all of your pride and strength.

She took all your joy and peace,
Now 40 is nothing
But your remedy.

Around That Time (Sonnet 18)

Oh wow,
Shall you?
Compare to the June and July?

From the dropping of the moon,
Til the end of sunlight?

Comparing two as discrete,
As can be.

She was temperate.
And I guess you loved testing her,
To see just how high her temper gets.

She was like the sun,
Too hot.
Both physically and mentally.

And when her days measured,
Ticks to the tock,
You can see her losing memory.

I mean she started acting differently,
Cold nights and she sipped the tea?
Excuse, the no visiting,
But she just had to grow up,
To see it in her own eyes,
That followed what a vision means.

Young Shaker,
You compare to compromise,
The setting of a younger life,
You ripe the fruits that grow,
Because you know,
She's quick to peak behind-

Seasons, she'll be screaming soon,
And yes she will be leaving you,
Compare her to the summer days,
And everything shall be okay.

And Then...

And then he said,
"Love is not love."
Which meant love never hopes for change.

He said,

"When it let go, then comes back like karma on a good day,
It should have never been left alone."

He said that if love was solid,
It never bent.
It could never break.
So that, if it were to ever change; it was never real.

So that, if love dies; it had never lived
So that, if it is to ever alter,
When alternations come along,
Peek A Boo,
The untold was more than a twisted truth.

He told us, "Love is not love"
Which made the young minds second guess,
So that, if love were to ever break your heart,
You know that it wasn't love,
It was you-

Bending its meaning out of place,
You, that misunderstood,
You, that held no value.

"Thou shall not direct one's misery at love's name"
If dedicated, we can change what love is equal to.
But always remember young one,
Love does not creep, nor change, nor fade,
If you do not allow it to.

Love is such (Sonnet 105)

Young Shaker,
I do not intend to recall,
Idols or vital recitals...

Where praises engrave,
As of tomorrow,
In our mind,
We sleep in excellence,
Like a lovely experiment,
Gone wrong.

It's not bad that my poems have the same meaning,
I'm saying the same things,
I'm just writing for freedom,
I let my love out,
Because I know someone is reading.
And someone is feeling,
Like feeling like,
They aren't needed.

And I know,
You're full of kindness,
Truthfulness,
Faithfulness,
You're taking this,
Making sins more of your daily routine,
You're moving.

I don't really know where you're going,
Neither for I,
So I meet you halfway with a rhyme.

Living alone,
But someone else is feeling the feeling.
All alone – to the third degree,
So I yearn for peace,
In the same invention that you had spent,
For love to be kind,

Divide to use as an instrument,
And you shall feel praised.

So much of,
More of that search in love,
Love is such.

Why Fear? (Sonnet 145)

Shaker,
I've been spying with my little eye,
A little picture that illustrates an illusion,
There's beauty in it – yes,
Though its purpose is prudence,
Allowing those to see growth,
Without seeing confusion.

They think they know what I'm doing,
Who I'm loving,
The direction I'm moving in,
Instant slips can affect one who's innocent,
And later that energy will just turn into ignorance.

Shaker, they swear there is a title,
But listen,
I know it's more of a thrill inside of a feeling,
Why can't we be chilling?

Why does the painter close the windows?
You see those – people see our picture start peeling.
The surface of things are fading,
And everyone is creating-
An image they say that couldn't be stationary,
And that's scary.

Why should I fear showing my picture?
There's delight in my piece,
I know what they peep,
But peeping to me don't mean a thing.

I spy with my little eye, something to keep.
I'll let them have it,
They can only draw a love that they see.

My love is forever,
My love doesn't fade.
My picture is eternal,

My image stays,
My picture is present,
It's the message of today,
It was better yesterday?
Nah, my picture always slays.
So when you're with me,
Let's grab the brush and smile as we paint.
From your mouth,
You created a beast that is fearful.

I'm the goon that still glooms,
After disaster is fed to me,
From your spoon.

That beast, had a heart like a hummingbird,
So yes her words hurt,
But I listened and never heard,
I listened and never earned,
Connections,
Those keys were my lessons,
To you, I promise I never learned.

Sometimes, you used that beast,
To satisfy my needs.

That same beast said,
"Not you" meaning "just leave"
And that, is the beast who,
Never slips in her tracks,
She's sophisticated,
I opened up my hands to her laugh,
And then she spit a burning verse,
What a lovely attack.

She was beast, and I saw the beauty,
She threw me the shade,
So I stopped looking for myself,
And watched myself walk away.

You know, sort of like you Shaker. What am I sposed' to do? Hate her? I ain't no hater like you Shaker. You made her, chide that tongue so much it was fun, so much that she took you on a trip in her dungeon. And that beast, made you live in her dungeon. And that beast, made you forget - in her dungeon. Lunging for choices to maximize the rusted. Dextrinizing happiness and loving how love hit. Until you came back to your combat sense, you never really knew what true love meant.

So you told a funk story just to tell me this. And I took your pain - so that I can tell these kids. We aren't loving. We're living in a Magic Land. We're happy, then sad, then we're happy again. We can't even feel the feeling with confidence. It's very dense - in the friend - that we sink - for benefits. This is bitterness. This is doubled up. This is 'keep the hope' just to give it up. This is luck for humans. This is very stupid. This is why I can't sleep at night. This is confusing. This isn't love. This is a vision. This is false, we don't know what we are really missing. We're missing ourselves.

Last Time (Sonnet 152)

You can't really say you really want me.
Say you're thinking of me…

So to make you better,
I blinded myself.
I knew who you truly were.
Swearing my oaths,
That you wouldn't swear.

> *I'm only doing this to help you,*
> *I don't need help.*

These promises are provocative and they prevail.
So what you saying?

It's like the game isn't the same,
We're fiddling pain,
At the tip of our fingers fixing the strange.

> *We swearing to our hallucinations,*
> *Hallelujah.*

We're dying for attention,
Swearing to spend our visit,
Collective, calm, and cautious,
Don't that sound like we're chilling?

This is just the night where we fly out business,
We had no business getting in,
We should've just stayed as friends.

Oh my goodness!

The Last Letter, Pal.

I don't think my mama,
Will be happy that I'm talking to you.
But I don't do this for her,
And I don't do this for you.
I don't do this for anonymous lovers,
Undercovers,
Young sisters touching brothers,
Its cause my days are blue.

It's not even that you've passed away,
I still feel you crying in heaven,
Writing all your pains away.

They say in heaven there is no weep,
Well, how you feel?
That lover you loved,
Is someone you will never get to see?

I mean, she has to be in hell by now?
Like how, does the woman,
Who put us through it?
Get to live in the clouds?

As many times,
As she had us drifting around,
In Magic Land wondering,
How we could find ourselves,
How- in the heck of it – will she settle in?

I know you two don't dance in the mansions,
Mashing for romance,
Handling those gasps,
Because you're tired of crashing.

Young Shaker,
I know - in one way - you hear me,
I know in two ways you can really feel me.

Yo, I hear you when I read about the pain you took,
And through what I'm feeling,
I feel it as I write this book.

This is for you. I'll keep your messages alive. Your work is forever amazing and taught all around the world. Thank you for teaching us about the dark side of love from a male perspective. This chapter is dedicated fully to you. My pleasure, young rose.

Part Seven: Plus Que Ma Vie (More Than My Own Life)

Heaven

Royalty

New Slaves

Assisi

Black Skinhead

Lungoteve x Leonardo

Oh, God

P.I.M.P

Universal Version

Stracciatella Mountains

Touchdown

Farowzie

Outro

When I was sixteen, my best friend had gave me one of the craziest ideas. We were walking through the halls at lunch on a random day of our sophomore year. We had both just got out of class and we noticed some flyers around that were hung up on other classroom doors. Something told the both of us to check out the flyers posted. Some of them were just weekly announcements that our schools ASB had posted, but one special flyer had caught my eye. It said, "2014 Spring Break Europe Trip."

At first it was just an idea that we fantasized about. She said, "T, oh my, man if we went to Europe..." and I actually stopped and gave it a closer look. I searched for more details to see how we could turn that little dream into a reality. She had traveled all over the United States, but all I've ever been was to South Carolina, where my mother's side of the family is from, and Los Angeles, CA where I have family stationed also. The flyer read that the trip was going to cost around $3,500. In the back of my head I knew that my family couldn't afford it. I just held the flyer and imagined what it would be like to leave my hometown and travel the world for the very first time.

A couple days passed and I had totally forgotten all about the trip. Later that weekend, it was my brother's birthday. My two best friends, Dajah Williams and Marcella Brown had come to celebrate. It was a nice day at the beach with all of my family and my parents were talking to my friend Dajah's mom. I had forgot all about the Europe trip until I overheard both my mom Dajah's mom talking about it.

My mom had called me over and brought it to my attention, she asked me, "So you were thinking about going on this trip to Europe? For 10 days at that?" I just smiled. I didn't know what to say. If the price wasn't so expensive I would've definitely remembered to ask her about it. I finally replied with some excitement, "Yeah. Dajah and Marcella want to go too." My mother just stared at me laughing and said, "Well, you all are gonna have to do some extra work for this to happen." And so we did...

Unfortunately, my best friend didn't get to go on this trip because she ended up moving back to her place of residence before she came to California, which was Cleveland, Ohio. Marcella, on the other hand, had the chance to work and raise enough money so that she could get this once in a lifetime traveling opportunity.

When my mother put down the first deposit for the trip and my teacher Mrs. Dagman told us that the money deposited is non-refundable, that's when I knew that I was going to go on this trip. I started off with only about $200. When my mother said that I would have to work to get the money to fund for my trip, she meant it. I was on my knees sweating in the sun doing garden work to earn the money that it took.

I wrote letters to my church and other organizations such as Kiwanis and NAACP asking for donations to help support my funds. I participated in a fundraiser that worked like this: I'd bring in an extra-large trash bag full of shoes. Each pound of shoes I brought in, I was given fifty cents to help fund my trip. I took in so many shoes that I had the most donated out of all participants of the fundraiser. I even gave some of my own shoes away to be sent to a charity in Africa. If you know me personally, I love shoes and I have a huge collection.

It is important for me to write about this specific act because it took me a while to figure out what I was truly doing. I wasn't just giving shoes to the less fortunate, I was sacrificing some of my possession to one day live out my dream. The very first day that I saw that flyer about Europe, I truly did not believe that I was going to go because of the price. What I learned from this story was to never doubt myself.

This was one of my first experiences in life where I had realized that when you want something in life, if you really want it, you will do whatever it takes to get it. Throughout the monthly payments for my trip, sure, I sometimes didn't think that my family couldn't afford to get the money in on time. I prayed to God to bless me financially and for him to please not close the door that I was so close to walking through. That was when I realized that I had to do one more thing before God was going to let me go. I had to know and truly understand my purpose for leaving.

For the whole month before Spring Break, I prayed to God to reveal to me my purpose and show me what my true reason to go to Europe is. After some weeks of prayer I began to open my eyes and see the true answer.

My goal on my trip to Europe wasn't to only have fun, learn historical facts, try new foods and shop all day. My goal was to find myself. God's spirit told me that his world stretches as far as it does from one ocean to another and sometimes it takes for a person to go and see what he has created in another city, state, country, or continent, to really find themselves. God had revealed to me how beautiful life really is.

When I was in Europe, I wasn't thinking of having much fun and going crazy in the streets like in the movies. I was thinking about coming back home to San Diego to tell the people that I had grown up with all of my life, that there is more to life than just living. I never knew what that truly meant until I got on that airplane and saw how beautiful God's creation is. Even though I was on a whole new side of the world, I still knew that I was sent by God and that I was living in a world that God controls. Since then, I have been thankful for everything that God blesses me with. I am more respectful to the earth that he created. For if I had not ever gone on this trip, I would still just be "living".

Today, I am doing much more than just living. I am loving. Loving God, and loving myself.

Intro

A rose once told me that I was its inspiration,
I blossomed after its coming just to be opposite.
Not knowing that those footsteps set were so positive,
I swallowed my own prerogative,
Then scripted scenes of silent sins,
Choreographed mental love steps in the name,
Wandering aside the flames,
To change perspectives due to royal imaginations.
There is no challenge,
But to balance
Beauty and BMWs,
When Love and Lamborghinis tie with everything that's become from you.
And beautiful descriptions,
Are listed by everyone but you.
In London,
Women tune out accents, and then hookah blooms out,
Passive aggression, passing pathways near adolescents
Homeless, near the Romans, near Paris' famous photos,
Near the David, near the chapel,
Near Cathedrals, there is a battle.
Silver spoon little riches,
Starving kids in the same city,
Remained
While all along the angels whistled my name
I was dreaming in the day,
While I made a decision
To write it down,
While in the towns
So I can make a difference
Share art through my eyes
And hope that it can inspire
Whoever
Decides to read this project...
To understand with precision
That there is more than life
Than just...
alarm clock goes off
This is for you
Him
Her
And them...

#oneLOVE

Takeoff

My mind, is far settling on heavy clouds
Floating in the winds
Who cares if my mind is up when I'm staring down?

Turbulence never shook a plane so hard that it could,
Shake and flatten my heart simultaneously,
I flew in the footprints of angles feet
I'm ashamed to say, I never prayed for the fantastic
But it happened

Today is my father's birthday; how could I be so dull?
So full of "I don't know how to feel" feelings
Filling my flesh from the dents in my skull
Would it be crazy if I asked God to pull plugs?
And tug on my arm to keep me focused
To properly grow like a lotus
And propose to the rose-like birds floating in the winds

Father, lately I've been dying in the mirror
My soul begs to differ; I'm mourning for an adventure
Excuse me as I kiss the...
Sweet pacific oceans before my pupils see missions
Excuse me as I visit...
Paradise

Father, let me wander, come and meet me in the night
I've been flying over sights I've never seen in my life
Time, is nothing
It's the time of my life and it's present
It's your present
I'm the closest to you that I've been in forever
I'm the closest to quick seconds away from heaven
I'm waiting,
For angels to lose pride
Stare me in the eyes at the gates...
Even if I can't get in-

Escort a young lord before the doors of golden gates
I pray,
Soon enough,
I'll smile and watch the angles play
Right here

High

I'm speaking to God more than I ever have…
How could this even be possible?
How did this come in the making to even be optional?
Was it all in your plans for me?
Or, is it all still a dream?

I'm just focused on getting high and away
To rewind to the stages of depression
And fast forward to when I learn valuable lessons
Father, I've been stressin'
Second guessing my faith; now molded in place
So if the face of Paris turns me to your will,
Then I'll prepare before the meals, prayer and meditation,
Facing every fear if it means coming near
Whatever that's in his guidelines
I find this very life changing and beautiful

I knew it though…
I knew I'd come so close and decide
I knew that one day I'd finally realize
How "REAL" life could be
I'm seeing life in different shapes
Ha ha, your highness,
I'm flying on clouds without my silver cape
When awake, I swear I'm dreaming
When dreaming, I swear I'm screaming
Help!
I'm lost in journeys
Equivalent to more than life itself

Golden Hour Glass

Spheres of excitement measured as they fall
Very slow as they toast another for growth,
But you know how coldies get in the spring

"Everything's been fine though"

Everything was golden leaning in my hour glass
In the past
Comfy and cuddled up right before they crash
The ugly bubbles laugh
In oblivious manner,
"Man, that's cray"
But, anyway,
I've been sippin' blood
Poured to the tip of my cup
Mama told me what was up
And now I know...
I never should've swallowed this much
Pain and excitement,
I've been choking on my reminded scenes of pleasure
Floating, as if my density, equaled feathers
Meanwhile,
I'm over skylines reclined in leather
Watching my ego and pride hop on my strings to fester

Not sure if it's measured soon or to be forever
But whatever
Creation should have no limits
This poison that I'm sipping on
Is wonderful
Don't burst the bubbles
Sizzling E under my thunder coat
Float
Don't mind me...
Just pour me another ounce
Bounce...
Back to life...
Back to the present time

Crucify Me

I can't recall the last time I...
But all I know is I'm at my highest currently
No birds, no bees, in my way
Premium isn't appetizing anymore
I'm just in the sky burning free

I am no eagle, no hawk, and no green parrot in the dark
Just a glooming soul
Yes, I've been plotting on the low...
My soul hides underneath my coat before my throat
Near a demon and a goat teasing
"I dare you to try and scream, T"
That's not the point though

The point is I'm in the sky burning free
Next to black stars and galaxies,
Milky ways that I can't eat
I wouldn't flee, if you knew exactly how it felt to be...
One in my eyes whispering you do **NOT** know the things...
But have attempted...

But hey, it all happens for "A
Reason", that deep stroked his fear to give it a tummy tuck
He doesn't agree with the philosophies of luck,
For adventure,
Brings him closer to greater tons of wisdom
Whether it be emerald,
Or silver dimes in the mind
I still can't recall the last time I...

Heard em' say, tomorrow holds a promise
A promise to be astonished and awed by human flaws
Brutal sins
How'd you get so thick?
By any means, If I vamped inside your cheeks,
Would you reach the peak of enlightenment?
Find excitement in an environment of sick and tiresome sentences?

Righteous, write this with your eyes closed
And wires wrapped around your metacarpals
So when life starts hurting
You'll prove every sentence is worth it
When your high, to everyone, just isn't working
Love your craft through verses, express to all, you deserve it
Don't stir the truth on purpose, unlearn it
Don't be nervous, but...
Though shall not lie

And I can't recall the last time I've been proud in myself
Only proud when it helps, heal
Can't remember the last time advice really healed
By shielding old feelings from battle scars steady bending off
Happy is temporary
I can't remember a time when deep breaths didn't scare me
I was once on the verge of falling free, merrily
On purpose, I proposed to fantasies, hoping she'd marry me

Now ever since she's came - it's been the dine of the decade,
Lit dining rooms with conversations - connected through straight faces
But hey, there's no time to trust pretty girls anyway

I can't recall the last time I...
But all I know is I'm at my highest currently
No birds, no bees, in my way
Premium isn't appetizing anymore
I'm just in the sky burning free
Soar with me,
If not, drop your fantasies from the top with arthritis
And high hopes of re-shining after illumination
Get high, off the supply that my mind is brutally laced in
And kiss me when I'm a vacant-soul at peace
Pre-game plotting under the pavement

Was it worth it? Would you do it again?
Climb to the top of the towers
Drop "To the Fifteenth Power"
Stating the leash was then broken and happiness was the token

We abused, and kissed everything in the air that was closest, to
nothing
Except God

It's burning, will you take me?
We can make love with the world but then you'd abort the baby
So what's the point little lady?
Be bold and crucify me
Everything inside of me is pressed down deep within my writings
Rewind to the era when breath taking was exciting
Soak it in and don't remind me

"You'll be fine, T"

Remember?

Separation

Where is the separation from man to God?

When do the right hands painted wrong become odd?
When does passion pinch perspectives like two peas in a pod?
When do mankind broad shoulders define his image? Pause...

La Vanta, art in atmosphere known as top notch
Angelo dropped Michael's thoughts,
In Motown,
With a lover plus an anonymous baddie who loves to go round
No Mona,
      "Young Lisa, it was very nice to meet ya,
    See the semen on your lips, no kisses, you're just a teaser
        I'm a grownup."

How dare one show up striking poses?
Bowing down to flowers near provoked and broken roses
I've proposed close to each and every sculpture
With calves showing
Illustrating the Sistine chapel on marble
I plead,
I planted the stars and fur de lise's

I planned, to put the angels next to demons
Forming hot flames on winter leafs
So fires within my eyelids would agree to leap and leave
I put the demons penis on anaconda vangs,
Due to inflictive reasons,
Never intended to spill the cherished golden secrets
Man, I slaughtered the gold in the cremated cerebrums
Then I swallowed to gulp, what my past never believed in

Half of a heart snatched and illuminated
Slowly showed that half of Gods brain, is ours
So we slid down towers downtown from led showers as cowards
And near each hour we spaz out shouting
        "Don't test GOD"

Since when did the right hands painted become odd?
From the beginning, if man was never in the image
Then who was to spare the rod?

Where were the children of mothers, when other species,
Came before Adams rib to create a human being?
Hmmm
From illustrations, Adam came from umbilical cords
So that leads us thinking that women where the first dirt lords
We came from dust...
I traveled miles with illusions to be confused in all I trust
God says that Adam was the first on earth to become
Angelo painted Adam with a bellybutton
Who, what, how, which one was pregnant?
Who was second? I guess this means,
You peep the secrets when you pay attention
I guess this means that - we will keep on second guessing
Art, and its definition plus its double sided message

When do the right hands that have been painted wrong become odd?
When does passion pinch perspectives like two peas in a pod?
When do mankind shoulders define his image? Pause...

I figured in awe, that Roman gods are never to be trusted
I stole the art and dusted gold paintings before they rusted
Trust in, God's word only.

Rozay & Roxanne

Now that I've been to London
I can tell you how I snuck
Inside the restaurant while Estefan slipped wines into his carry on
While baby had a back frame like Barry Bonds
She hit it out the park and turned heads before she talked
All the men knew that her head game was way too strong
And she was silent,
Til Rosie put the poison aside her bedframe
Two men couldn't fit, but twenty were on her membrane

Roxanne, Roxanne,
May I have this dance and let romance fill the night?
Chardonnay grapes and Rozay, two attractions before her eyes
Subtract the past, from lips to hips, an instant enterprise
Until they realize, love in the city of London
Is redundant
When women willingly sleep with anything that will come in

Roxanne, Roxanne,
Where are you taking me?
Break me off so we can vacate into the maple suites
Maples get tastier by her naval, so remake the cream
And when the angels beat, the doors down
Suddenly blood drips quick to the floor now
She smiles and calls you the beater,
Screaming you're the "Caesar" in her world
So before he grips his zipper attempting to leave the doors
Threats over his neck, unaware of the storms
Sex in the city - can leave - the sheets warm
His dome piece screaming "peace" while he's stuck in a dorm

HIV
Mama said, wait until I crave the ring
I've proposed to live it up
With Roxanne living in my dreams
In my head
Yes, her head game - way too strong
As I stare into this wine glass,

She comes politely asking, for my presence on the floor
To dance, I contemplate and concentrate
Just before I vision sins and get the proper chance
She yanks my handkerchief...

Roxanne, Roxanne, Where are you taking me?

Oh, Londonium

                                        Little high, Little ho'
                                        So far we go

Ash colored mini birds painted with tar and snow
They touched my soul...
Somehow

Oh, Londonium
You've given excitement and pandemonium
The closest thing to opium,
Would fail to lift me to these skylines

You are filled with forest green Hyde Parks
Piccadilly planted perfect pictures just to restart, life.
I've learned that you are thousands of years old,
Still firm and bold
Golden bridges never even came close to being frigid
No matter when tempted, you never fell down to a wind
When did they come up with the riddle?
London Bridge is falling down
You turned my life upside down
Great Britain

I never knew you were so similar to Rohr
Crossed over underground like subways in New York
It's amazing how you move forward;
When we bring back the past.
You shine as we laugh transforming our hearts under masks

                                        Little high, little ho'
                                        So far we go

St. Paul Cathedral
Stands tall reconstructed from smoke
So we deep throat the victory that floats due to history
And Big Ben ticks Hickory-Dickory-STOP
Listen to Mother Nature make a symphony
I promise I'm not singled out to hearing songs unwillingly
Just as I remember you,

I pray that you will remember me
You've been amazing

Oh, Londonium
Thank you, for the joy that you bring
I promise to you,
My return is coming soon.

Homecoming

Do you think about me now and then?
What if today was the day I put down the pen,
To ask what is my purpose when I start to mix my past within
My present, are these gifts, blessings, or lessons?
I'm coming home.

Maybe we can make it back to Rome.
Roaming and wandering
Honoring the fact that it's all mental
Picking at the thorns, cutting straight through our potential
Mistletoe kisses on Christmas, yeah, we missed those.
But it's never too late, I appreciate the thought.

It's not too late to get a French kiss, is it?
Maybe we can give Paris a visit?
Wait a minute let it pivot in your pupils
We could gather Euros
Exchange for high fives and koodos
But who knows...

Maybe we can start again?
It wasn't hard to stay faithful to the royalty
When loyalty, crossed my mind at the gorgeous feet
Of David
And Michelangelo's master paintings,
Maybe we could rewrite the ancient.
So in Hollywood, our names...
Engraved to the pavement,
Lost inside a lonely star, that's what we are.

Maybe, you'll be patient?
Or maybe I'll be racing to paste myself while breaking,
Off the branches and jumping out of the nest
Maybe we could backtrack to the best, times of our life.
If you don't know by now, I'm talking about the nightlife.
Skylines in London; rain to keep us running,
The highs that take you nowhere near California kushes

Maybe we can get high, naturally?
As long Black & Mild's and blasphemy,
Don't exist.
Maybe we can resist the temptation,
And kick hesitation out the way?
Maybe, I'll bring you back with me one day.

Do you think about me now and then?
What if today was the day I dropped the pen,
Would you care for my experience?
Or laugh until delirious,
Will you still take me serious?
I've been chewing the same thoughts since December,
And I'm still curious
Will you listen if my voice isn't clear enough?

Well anyway, I'm coming home
Tell the world that I'm coming
Tell my family - every smile I put on,
I was bluffing.
Tell my cousins,
I miss when all we had was time to laugh,
Now we pass each other up to rest instead.
No unity
Tell them I watched the living room cartoons
And found Scooby Doo's mystery
All alone
Because everyone else was "grown"
Tell my father I made it on my own
I'm in France
Throwing keys inside the river with my mind
Instead of hands
Check that equation
Basketball at home
Near my scooter in the basement
I just wanted to get away
Elevate as gravity swishes
Here comes the relay of the decay
That's been dropping me whole life
Can you relate?

No, Mama I'm coming home.
I'm just sitting at the top of world
All alone
Never, will I ever
Come again to watch the throne
That is equal...
To me...
Vomit over my ego
Tell them
That I didn't miss them when I was gone
I missed them
All along, when I was sitting at home.

Gorgeous

Ain't no question if I want it, I need it.
You can sleep but I'll be dreaming, with open eyes gleaming.
And I've wrote every single pinch of my reasons,
Heard the devil screaming, it takes much to keep me beat defeated,
I'll never walk this earth skipping with frowns staring down.
Just for another man's smile.

Not for nothing in my pathway of alpha
I'm no coward I'll keep climbing each hour,
To flower blossomed visions,
And scatter every intention,
To taste a raindrop from heaven and to tell my daddy I did it,
I will never ever live to let him down, down, down...

It started in all my classes after two passes,
The passion that grew from whiplashes and flashbacks of Samuel
Nothing I couldn't handle,
But handle bars of life came loose.
I was battling gravity ever since I came through, wires.

How could I move on with reminders near my eyelids?
Was I supposed to deny or forget it to pass by it?
From slow beats to passed down genes of bronchitis,
I stole maidens to make my last name shine where the light is.
When no one in our family decided to make it viral,
I made it, how it feel to see your 3rd nut shining?
Redemption, I won't slip I'm so close to your fingertips,
I'm so close the angels praising, just waiting to let me in.
I'm so close to heavens gates I see the gold so I won't peek,
I just write until these lines elevate me to my peak.
I'll keep writing thoughts down while I'm riding in the clouds,
I'll sacrifice my smile
If it means I'd make my daddy proud.

Ain't no question if I want it, I need it.
You can sleep but I'll be dreaming, with open eyes gleaming.
I wrote down every single pinch of my reasons,

Heard the devil screaming, it takes a lot to keep me beat defeated,
I'll never ever
Let you live this down, down, down.

Is "New slang" replacing "New slaves" intelligence?
I'm battling correlation with relatives and irrelevance.
But I never lost sight of who the soul inside of Terrance is.
More than life itself, imperatives for my palindrome
My heart beats in awe from the gorgeous glimpse I've kissed on.
I've been sleeping in the same bloodstreams that I slipped on.
I knew I should've listened; I was 6 but didn't get it,
I see beauty for what it is now, so in my mind, I bend it.
And that's the beauty of having the brain of a soldier,
I carry the peace in my eyes, and keep his pain on my shoulders.
I never knew that love would come before I got "older"
But I'm older now, and somehow to indefinite, I'm sober.
I'm closer to my dreams near the storms and tsunamis.
Whoever said I couldn't get to heaven in my Maserati,
McLaren, Lamborghini or a baby blue Bugatti?
I guess you missed it in description, pretending as if you saw me.

Ain't no question if I want it, I need it.
You can sleep but I'll be dreaming, with open eyes gleaming.
I wrote every single pinch of my reasons,
Heard the devil screaming, it takes a lot to keep me beat defeated,
I'll never walk this earth skipping with frowns staring down.
Just for another man's smile.

I've been riding round' getting it, listening to voices.
I made Sammy HAPPY on his birthday, that's important.
Pouring feelings in golden glasses on jets screaming "Jordan"
The good life, I don't need mirrors for it.
It's gorgeous the way I see, you'll never understand,
Until your mind comes to blink, sins away.
I pray, that you'll dream with eyes open.
Bloom like a lotus and promise to the depths to stay devoted.
I love you, in your eyes I'm only hoping.

I've creeped behind the scenes and kneeled at the cathedral.
I've mistaken brown pigeons for fearless eagles,

I've been in Italy, with bickering tendencies,
And a memory, based on a lack of painkiller remedies.
I've pushed with little energy; I've looked within the history.
And the only thing that I found was clearly down in me. Art.
Enlightenment stages, I found in the dark.
Locked, behind the curtains in my heart
No sparks
I am...

   Not for nothing in my pathway of alpha.
   I'm no coward I'll keep climbing more hours,
     To flower blossomed visions
 And scatter every intention, to taste a raindrop from heaven and to
     tell my daddy I did it.
  I will never ever live to let him down, down, down...

Heaven

Have you ever been to heaven?
Have you ever
Bowed in the presence of invisible power?
Or believed before the towers?
Have you kneeled at the gates?
Have you ever...

Gripped dreads tied in unity 'til the oil
Runneth over and boils,
Slowly turning to liquid
Have you sipped it?
And do you know just how it tastes?
Have you crouched beneath doubts with piped down attitudes?
Have you, ever...

Kneeled at the gates to replace,
Pride and gain understanding
In the midst of motion finding yourself grasping "LIFE"
Have you felt the pain while rain,
Came from where the man reigns
Angels sang, melodies and tears hit the golden gates
What a shame, as it entered the entrance of Versailles
What's a scream to a sigh?
sigh
When only kings can make it out alive...

Have you ever stopped to accept the raffle?
Fifteenth Power vs Sistine Chapel
Now that's art...

Covered in humanity wrapped in silken gavels
When they fall they call the name
Broken hearts reveal the secrets
None are breathing
But all become praised
Man's perception is ugly and it uses love in vein
Have you whimpered and wiped your heavenly tears away
With thorns,

Cover your face you are not a young lord
You are vacant
To heavens limitation
Impress the fun in Satan
Have you slept on sheets built in hells basement?
No.

Royalty

I've never seen a diamond jump from hell
I've kissed the ruby on the promise rings,
Please don't tell
Though I'm not scared of adventures
In the turn up town
Walking with mistresses with percentages
0.08 plus over in the system full of liquor
Creating chemistry, obliviously
We don't care

McLaren's and Maserati's
Metros and paparazzi
Opium and that oxy
Ashtrays destroying the body
Straws to sip Vodka
Glasses to gulp Bacardi
Probably rushing to fulfil dreams toasting one in the air
Running to race our dreams screaming "We don't care"

We're riding strollers on the magnum opus
Happiness and violence
Equals money, that's the token
Flick lighters, next to lions, with the liars, near the heem
Who cares to die when angels arrive right before we dream?
Ask Leonardo

Chardonnay and champagne by the plates laced with escargot
That's the motto
Get wasted or die trying
Nothing strong enough to hit the spot
So we hold tight to the bottles
If sex is a remedy, automatically you're a model
With pretty titties and a heart that's better hallow
                                           Now that's deep
What separates a woman on man's tongue, from a queen?
If he thinks, "Hmm, she moans, I bust, and out the door, I leave"
Paint her on paper porn and figure "Hmm, I'll name her Mona
Lisa"

A woman is royalty,
Because all between her legs, is all that equals man's kingdom
Lisa, you ain't dead
I can hear your heart beating
Slowly as it's boiling
I realize you are royalty

I've never seen a diamond jump from hell...

New Slaves

Now I'm headed back to Rome
Pompeii was dope
I know a pretty place where K9s make your pockets broke
My mama was raised in the era when...
Life wasn't near excellent...
Money and fashion wasn't so relevant...
So let me clear...
My throat

They say slavery don't exist
We cop Gucci belts from 2 to 6 hundred
It's lack of intelligence
To say that we are no longer lashed by the whips
Red Octobers on silver sofas
Smell the aroma welcomed in Roma
And feel needy to gather leather and Jordan merchandises
So Instagram likers can like us
And comment on the prices
If it's cheap, then our life isn't exciting

We just want a Picasso
We love to glance at the flashes capturing the models
We love to say that life is precious
We blow our dough on dosha
And think about college - second
Oh boy

They try to tell me that slavery is gone
Behold the models before cameras on the newest iPhone
We adore
And we don't care to be the best generation
That's why the ignorant stars are all the most famous
We've became adapted and trippy-drunk off the basics
Dummy lit in the clouds, now afraid to hit the pavement
We don't care for statistics
We don't care where they place us
We don't care for when grandma said only Jesus can save us
We care about Nike, Jordan, Adidas, and then the rest...

Is why we leave America to blow money in Paris

And they say slavery don't exist...
When to society I am still that menace
Independent in euphoria
I'm walking in the store with ya'
Ya' owner watching – and it's pathetic

And it won't get better on its own will it?
Independent in euphoria, you see me as a menace
To society I blend in
Sobriety in my system, I admit it
I'm addicted
A victim inside this prison
No pilgrim
I'm still spending my soul
To stay fitted
Aren't you...

One of the new slaves, too?

Assisi

Right here, it's like California's December
Winter weather, a winner holds golden euro's for gelato
A fraction to America is a tease
The pigeons fly different than V formations in cities
Sing, little hummingbird, sing the melody

Delivered loaded tons of respect filled to the "T"
Royal when it falls before Christ
Sphere, cone, or stripe, roll sins down tonight
As long as the circle crashes at the head of the cathedral (heathen people)
Without a puff of the herb or injection of the needle
Liquid

Right here, eyes glow in the sun like angels,
For awesome sights become vivid
Indecisive minds running for the islands
With liars and lions chasing
They praise for the reminder, that it's not easy to be righteous

Right here, is when hymnals are the only power sirens
They swim in wine bottles to gulp the tears from their eyes,
And she, will hand Lucifer viruses,
If his foot comes too close
Hang him with the ropes around the "PAX"
Watch his soul tumble - picking up speed - to collapse
Bound to crash at la primavera de montaña
Bashing his head on stones, for growth.
As long as the circle crashes at the head of the cathedral (heathen people)

Using the youth "x's" before calling adult "T's" steeples
No need for that opium or the needles
Assisi, is high enough for the geniuses
Blue skies; so garden snakes teal lies in the evening
Then rivers turn gold in the noon
Land of the mushrooms and silver spoons...
Assisi is righteous,

Even Satan was once "beautiful"

Right here, is where they misunderstood
The concepts
Therefore,
I told them
The word
Word.

Black Skinhead

This is for the roses
Negative one steady toastin'
Poison is potion, dried out and devoted
3:45 in the morning,
Lisa, throwing the plates
She's get crazy while deep in her zone man

Straight to the basement
Forget a replacement
Demons horny steady moanin'
So he goes in, yes
I believe,
Da Vinci was putting those strokes in
He beat it between every evening
Then painted the face
Just so people could notice

But uhhh...
I was just....
And you know this...

So throw on a black mask of illusion
Bow so hard that you feel foolish
Stroke on the top of a whisper
And laugh about stories of Jesus and Judas

Think of David
Think of shadows and movements of Satan
Think of every perspective mistaken
Think of self-expression underrated
From the basement

Follow me into the attics of steam
Close your eyes - gently listen to me
Your mouth is shut tight but I still hear you scream
We should've just settled in Rome
Alone and together,
Together alone

"Cause I can't handle hectic screams
Through the bass in my beats
So close your eyes
Slow down
And fall to your knees
Let your mind do its job, Praise God."

Lungoteve x Leonardo

I just stopped peeling wraps today
Sweet pieces full of horror,
Bronze bottles full of torture
I just dropped the famous magazine
Lisa in London steady cuffing drugs from her balcony
You mad at me?
Take it off!
That means the watches and the scarfs,
Every other piece of cloth
Cause I'm about to set it all, off.

Nudity, she is made from Marble not a two-piece
Leon, I know you were puffin' on that new leaf
Oo'wee, crumbled stones went right between your doobies
Lip prints missing from your kisses right between her boobies
Easy, "His" acts rated "R" before his "Toy"
She was the history in his mind before employed for sending joy
Painted with force and then rejoiced...

Just stopped peeling wraps today...
Think of entertainment
Mona Lisa grinding on the pavement
Then Da Vinci on his back masturbating
Now that's art... With lights dimmed in a marbled dark basement

Now the young lords sketch sex in the city
MAC, Chanel, and luxury handbags from Fendi
On the corners you'll fail to find a venue for feelings
They just smile at a masterpiece and find it quite appealing
When an artist of the century would find it quite offending
Cause art is the visible new beginning
Painted hopes of clean sins just to balance every remedy
Then throw them down the drains where the ugly rocks and pennies
sleep

Potentially pushing art away to flow in the rivers
I guess beauty wasn't worthy until delivered
I just stopped peeling wraps today

But all I do is litter
Emotions and perspectives
To teach the world many lessons
Poetry is an art – and easily it's my pleasure
I paint the pictures like Leon
I hope you peep the resemblance
I hope you see the difference, in Lungoteve and Leonardo.

Oh, God

Here we go again
Striving through the highways of weak rain in the winds
Fell in love with Prada and Gucci before I spent,
Time in museums, to focus on the meanings
I came a long way from golden hour glass meetings
At first, I just wanted to get the pieces,
Of peace

But peace, turned into turnt nights and no sleep,
Meaning my smile shattered quicker than five heartbeats,
In the center of London,
There's no time to dream,
Neither in Paris
People who act very happy - are truly careless
Young dogs puffing smog sticks, through the air
Chanting with chardonnay grapes in our spare-time

We throw our hands up high in the sky
Pouting...
Before you doubt it, at least give it a try
Before you cry remember why you smiled in France
Or die trying to pull euros out your stylish pants
Oh, God

Appalled, I can see how Yeezy is a...
Ranting blasphemy, from a balcony, breaking laws
King to a God, God to an unbeliever
Royal from Yeezy to Caesar, make life look much easier
Oh, God
Come spare the rod
For we do not remember the things – we never forgot

A collage of everything I've seen
Just wouldn't match my thoughts
I'm a genius fiend freezing demons in their demise
When the vicious go to sleep, I roar before the dawn
Pause

Hold close to your thoughts
Ignite the applause
And call out to God
For guidance
Oh, God, it's better if we stay silent
Correct me if I am not
One who never forgot.
The truth.

P.I.M.P

Cruising down the street in my...
Attire with some fire in my jeans (genes) over my eyelids
It's common
Don't put a comma to the drama that still runs on
Metro systems, I swallowed the stress at dinner
And saw Roxanne on a picture
At this fancy restaurant...
Crept around the corner and noticed every flaw
My fault, don't mean to shove
But I suffer memory loss
I stopped,
In the center of Oxford street with a sinner
A serpent, a new beginning, and a 20 in my denim
What I'm supposed to do?
Slipping on the corner, I remember this
This is Déjà vu,
Pleasure is in the mind
And pain arrived with the prostitutes

"There's a door in here,
You're waiting on a mission
To get you to your room"

It started...
We came together and partied...
You told me about your hobbies...
Then held my hand in the lobby...
You told me your sob story...
Then mixed it in the Bacardi
Sunshine, was near tomorrow
You said you'd stick to your promise...

"Forget about all the options...
Because you got me
Meaning it's yours as long as you want it...
Please answer, do you copy?"
Roger that...

"But if you get caught sweetie, you won't remember that,
You won't know your location; you're thinking you're still in France

You're dreaming in Assisi...
You forgot about the crash
So tender and soft, we talked, just as we danced
Into a new world
So welcome into this new world, Terrance...
Don't forget me; I hope - you know who - this is."

(Player In My Persona)
For short just call me a pimp.

Universal Version

Every breed of birds sings sweet songs
Brown pigeons watch the city like lions to the Safari
Graffiti from bubble gum to purple to Rastafari
Sorry,
More art in Paris and Italy than in Harlem
Daygo and Hollywood get high from lifting stardom
All the beautiful places...
We can make it
We just have to escape this garden
Barbed wire... surrounds

Sharp is the only wardrobe, Gucci is the product
Prada is the sister; Ralph Lauren is just the option
The North Face is adolescent's protection in the weather
Whether it's raining or not
Stop, to French kiss gypsies
Hiding behind disguises with red coin cones empty

Funny cause...
They won't even look you in the eye
Just hands and opportunity,
Hoping you drop your pride

Round n' around n' around, n around, we go....
City to city, anxious to portion parts prettier
Porsches and Sensimilli
Since its few, I guess we spend time to make a milli
Blow it in Paris burning rubber behind a Bentley, coupe.
It's funny what a dog will do...
For some kitty

This is where the teenagers get tipsy
Where the "friendly" steals your identity
For lime shots mixed in Henny
This is when the lonely roses just start feeling dizzy
Where violets peel their scabs
And dandelions keep wishing
Empathy and pity, is all that they will be getting, soon.
What am I getting myself into...?

Universal version

Stracciatella Mountains

Lounging in the clouds
Looking down on Dalmatian
Iceland before I hit Croatia

This is the predicament
When life is really a box of chocolates
And mama always liked those little candies
If she was on this plane with me,
I know that she'd be happy
But anyway,
Mom, you know you're here in spirit

So exquisite, so excuse me as I use my gift
To pivot awareness and blast off at intermission
I've never seen anything like this...
I've never been this excited...
I still can't recall the last time I...
Have been reminded
How beautiful life is, or how ugly the night gets
But the nightlife might just be head over the prices
Priceless days and night shifts
Can wipe you clean off all of the righteous-ness
Inside

How shall I rest above mountains in the sky?

In heaven - is where I - wish to reside
Never knew the blueprints
Of a mountain could kiss the fountains
Where imagination leaks in heavy ounces
Bounce

Chocolate chip chunks on ice cream Sundays
Dozing near citizens of Great Britain
Never knew that I would be drifting, living this life
Am I living it up?
Or just dreaming because...
It's real, but it doesn't feel real

Though it does…

Gelato spills from the tip of my cup
To the mountains
I've decided to move
Astounded
In God's plans.

Touchdown

From takeoff
I was only searching for the adventurous…
Statistics licking perceptions of all that it came to be
Well,
Europe sure has been good to me.
I've been in London with redundant lovers
And under covers with night terrors
But in the morning things went better as I moved on.
Off to Paris,
Where appearance is what seemed to be a soul's credential
I lost myself in my mental,
While dreams reeled me back in.
Skipped to Florence and headed to Rome
Roaming with gorgeous…
Walked in the Coliseum
With all the French girls screaming
In vein,

> "What is your name, where are you from
> Mention the reason, tell me please,
> Why have you come?
> Are you a singer, a rapper, what is your occupation?
> Quit playing. A Poet? I cannot believe,
> Two-three – selfie - can we take please?

And yeah, that's how Rome went…
Spent time out in Italy
That's where most of my dough went
The equalizer, the streets are so quiet
Something like Ratatouille
Instead, there's grown up movies
Every day, on the scene…

Made it to top,
Of the Eiffel Tower frightened, pursuing dreams
Got to Assisi,
Where the T's were crosses, burned by the castles
Like Jesus of Nazareth
Instead I held my pamphlet

Inside cathedrals, stared the volcano in Pompeii
I made it to the top all in one day.

                    "Mama I made the Touchdown"

But there's no place to celebrate, now.
Touchdown
I'm still wondering how
This all happened.

Farowzie

Farowzie, Farowzie
Forgive the opposing
But though shall not judge
For thou do not knoweth,
Just call them unknowing,
Floating minds sidetracked by demons
The heathens called your name, as you arose, peaking
At the mountain tops, we have not forgot your beautiful essence
The angles call you a blessing, for more than one reason
You are a star that shines

Natural beauty across the eyes,
As we all read and worship mentally
Farowzie, tears fall in memory
Of your nevertheless, pressed over precious tilt of a laugh
I remember you danced aside my hip and caught a grasp
Of friendship
Before we even awoke, before we even dreamt it
We left it, up at the mountain top
So that when it dropped,
We'd leave an unremarkable mark in the depths
Where X marks the spot, we crept in-to the webs
As two, and loved life, for the simple fact that we had
Each other, in one another's eyes
And now...

All I see when I see your face, is mine
Except I don't see you're smile,
I see the cries, of now and the future
Because now I have to do, without you...
Your love, about, in the atmosphere
The clouds, I will count
But will I, never be to find you, within
The winds

Farowzie, Farowzie
Forgive the opposing
But though shall not judge
For thou do not knoweth,

For they brought the bullets
Sending war to your heart
And now they weep only because they forgot
How important you are
You are a star that shines.

Dedicated to Rosemary Summers

Outro

Here, all that there is to do is wonder...
Plunder my goods
Steal goats from right under my hood
I said I'm going to look
Come back and have stories to put
In my youth
To release the truth
Give them every mystery,
And never speak of proof
Not to spook, but to inspire
Mental movements grooving
Through the wires
Life is nothing but a game,
Right?
Less than enough
More is expected
Full of contradictions
And pleasuring benefits
Stop and listen

Block a vision
Criss-cross broad intentions
And unlearn
The unseen
So you can speak
On what they never heard
What they never saw
Is all that I've seen
From the bachelor to the master
I've created a piece
For peace
Decreasing the issues
From every city that I skipped through
As a genius holding Ginsues
Cutting deep inside my rearview
Mirrors,
I did it so they'll remember
To pay attention next time
And Listen...
This is Art

Finally wakes up

To be continued...

Part Eight: Proverbs. Six. Sixteen

Haughty Eyes
Lying Tongues
Hands that **Shed** innocent Blood
A Heart that devises **Wicked** Schemes
Feet that are quick to rush into **Evil**
A false witness who pours out **Lies**
Ones who stir **Conflict** in the community

Haughty Eyes

What do you know about the haughty eyes?

Filled blatantly and disdainfully
With an arrogant demeanor
The Grinch and Grimreepers reflection
Masters attention
Lynching the subtle
Picking the naughty
Haughty eyes love running to-

Everything that God is resistant of
These eyes look down in shame,
And lustful demons pick them up
Simultaneously uplifting their souls
Turning their hearts cold
Folding, their minds into halves
To belittle themselves for everything in this world,
They know they can't have

Doing it, and doing it, and doing it... well
Blinded by ourselves
On a beautiful journey to hell
Up so high,
We forget about each and every time we fell
Haughty eyes,
Make us unable to see the thrill - out of sight,
Out of mind - we roll down the hills
With heads of steam
Reaching out to grasp anything-
Out of Gods space
Making us feel out of place

We're just saved,
And complacent,
With being sacred, sometimes.

So we search with our eyes,
Without a foundation,

And believe the unseen,
Scenery - in the making.

Lying Tongues

They say it all started from a serpent, in the dirt
Was the purpose, just to hurt us?
Would a serpent's slither make you feel a bit nervous?
If you were to blossom,
In a garden full of Gods most awe-some…

Tangled, twisted, and for the wicked,
Lies come frequently - as a nation we miss it
Despite the fact, we don't see liars in the mirror
You live behind the mirror

Just living,
Too focused on justice and liberty
Are you forgetting?
About God's word, the word that you heard, from the beginning of time

TELL ME YOU DON'T KNOW,
ACT AS IF YOU'RE SURPRISED!
TELL ME YOU DON'T KNOW,
LOOK IN MY EYES AND LIE!

We live in a world on two different axels
Where I cannot believe one word that you preach
For as whenever you speak,
I shall never know…
If your words are worth much, or unworthy

Are we worth each other's word?
I was told once, many other times I've heard,

Trusting in MAN, will only get you hurt.
Early - early in the morning I heard the birds sing,
And by their sweet tones of love,
They surely saved me.

From now on,
Bow on replenishing truths,
Right the wrongs,

I'll write sincere dedications for you…

Hands that Shed Innocent Blood

If you were to see, someone so innocent slowly passing away
Would you do whatever it takes, refusing to let a heart fade away?
Or would you…

Become an invisible soul in a city,
With angels that derived from hell?
Would you run from the angels?
Who would you tell?

Would you witness, pay attention, and clearly vision
The death of an innocent?

Trayvon Martin

Would your heart ease up or without a doubt or harden?
No matter the color of the face,
No matter the name of the race,
Would justice for the innocent be the only thing you chase?
If hands that shed innocent blood, cuddled a case?

If you knew the way it was drawn out,
Would you block out,
Your vision, to mention-

When they taught us about liberty and justice?

We have downfalls,
Innocent souls are gone
I don't understand it all
Where did it all go wrong?

Since when was there a reason to kill - for suspicion?
The color of the skin - isn't hidden
The moral of the story – is written
The idea of free will – misgiven,
Due to, the corrupted society that we live in.

May you Rest in Peace, Trayvon. We love you!

A Heart that devises Wicked Schemes

Point the barrel at his head
And don't give him time to blink
Don't give me too much time to think
As my heart bleeds, his bark screams
I don't breathe, he begs for mercy
I slow down, they code me
The devil provokes me
I give the last stare to my homies
I close my eyes, then slowly
Squeeze

Painted to the highest degree
Just you and me
Outdoors loving the sinful attraction,
Noises and scratches
Genuine actions,
We keep it active,
Moans of disaster,
Perfectly capture,
Then burn we keep matching.

King and a queen
Producing a fraction
Perfection
Receiving laughter followed with napkins
To clean the innocent blood shed after

Wicked Schemes, Wicked Screams, Wicked Dreams, Wicked
Things.
Wicked people, we are…

Feet that are quick to rush into Evil

Holding onto our vengeances, committing sins just to kiss revenge,
we ask the lord to give, give us mercy and forgive.

Forgive us for critical decisions, we see children, but we don't care
for keeping distance.

We keep living. We pull triggers, we can't figure, out the puzzles, we
remember, our own struggles

We lie, sin, and cheat.
And depend on God to always keep
His promises,
When we can't even keep one...
We use our haughty eyes to seek
Sin,
At ease we breathe as we sin,
Break commandments, and we treat his
Word as if doesn't mean...
To us

We are so quick to rush to evil
We pray for God to forgive,
And the next day we live the sequel
Be grateful...
That the Lord above is merciful...
Always know indeed you need him
Because if it wasn't for his mercy...
We wouldn't be running quick to whatever is evil

What am I trying to say is-
We wouldn't be here...

I'm not perfect,
I have quick feet
And it hurts me to admit.
Lord, forgive us, for our sins,
Though we treat you like...

Before we run too far...
And lock eyes with Satan,
Just know that we are not sacred, on purpose
On Sunday we worship
Your name,
Through the weekdays - we don't speak - on your name
I know it hurts, you're probably weeping from your window pane
Looking down - on your children - in nothing but shame...

Lord, forgive us, for our sins
We are just trying to live,
Not according to your will
But will,
You, be patient?

A False Witness Who Pours Out Lies

I read in a proverb,
A wicked man shuns evil
A wise man never lies
I also read, that real men never cry
I heard the birds singing - humans can't fly
That was like Jimi, excusing as he kissed the sky

Let's have a moment of silence
For the wicked ones committing the crimes
And the ones stand behind the line,
Of what trust really is.
The ones who open their mouths with fabrication,
And make us tune out everything they're creating,
And find it very fine to, lie to
Innocent souls that believe,
The devils' tricked mentality slicked under their sleeves

They wonder why - they never feel the wonderful breeze
Because a wise man shuns – through his lungs,
As we breathe

We wake to fabrication without leaning to truths.

A wise man fears the lord,
So why don't you?

You can sip all the poison,
But you can't harvest the fruit,
Spoon feed,
You'll build a village,
That will follow the truth,

You should tell it.

One who stirs Conflict in the Community

Riding around hesitant
Up to no good
Minds coated in irrelevance
Love in the hood,
They found it,
Loving the hood
I guess it just all sounded,
A little too… unreal

Still, they ride, they ride
Watching the girls hop scotch,
As time tick tocks
Watching out for cops across the bridges
Busting missions - cigarettes in the mouths of young souls
Headed south
Shadows of the wrong road – come close.

"Hey, silver spoon I know you come from ya-bish"
They sang it because they knew what it meant.

Another criminal stirring conflict
Around the corner peace sings up, and the spliffs
Get lit, and the minds get elevated high - no shifts
No grip, no clip, no sips, no Bloods, no Crips, just them
Boys on the bicycles who run the whole block.

Little Sammy got his bike snatched - went straight to the cops
And when the boys found out - it was back to the block
Sammy got knocked straight to the ground from his head with a rock.

Up to no good, the violence in the hood won't stop
And every life is in jeopardy till' the tick turns tock
Till the air collapses - till the sun turns black
They move the crack cocaine – cash can bounce right back
So, spread good news in a mad city - improving your acts
Cause with conflict, "LIFE"
*Is something you lose like **that!***

In the blink of an eye,
You'll lose an eye - to blink.
Riding round' hesitant,
Not attempting to think.
I opened my Bible scared to find the rival in me.
And saw everything God said - I could change for free
In Proverbs 6:16

Part Nine: Nineteen Roses
(Forever love waiting on you)

She
Let me clear my throat
Amaya
The Vent
Nineteen
Red are Roses
You & the Sins
Lonely Rides
Catch me if you can

The biggest communication problem is we do not listen to understand. We listen to reply.

She

I've been waiting on this love forever,
Right toe touching the pot of gold,
For the rainbows,
Tell me several stories.

I've been fortunate enough to put my pains before me,
I've been searching during sermons,
Hiding behind the curtains,
In other words,
Learning how to find the brighter side.

I've been staring at the sunsets,
Two tears, one smile,
One step, two texts.

Who's that girl?
I saw her walking in that blue dress,
Who's next?
Assuming - I put my life into that?

I've been living too black,
I see people kissing.
I shot my mom's with a needle,
Nobody paid attention.
What?

Look at what - that needle did to me,
It revealed frozen secrets as broken mysteries,
Nobody sees those.

My mama makes me smile the most,
But she can't even see that,

Cause I'm in here writing stories off her relapse.

I'm trying to fill this deep damped damn,
I've been swimming near the deep damns,
Now the waters' at my throat,
But you don't see that.

I've been searching for some voices,
Choosing to truce my choices,
I'm juggling my purpose with its importance.
You don't see.

I've been aborted,
Adopted by the rib with no judge,
They don't see,
All I screamed for,
Was forms of love.

I've been wasted,
Sleeping on the floor instead of my bed,
Cause I'm too scared that my head-
Will fill with more nightmares.

I'm so tired of this silly movie,
It's too confusing,
I'm conscious, walking straight,
Promising you - I'm moving,
But I don't feel I'm going anywhere.

Nobody even really cares,
Yo, why am I still writing this?

I guess it's time to do like Miley Cyrus did.
Come in like a wrecking ball,
I swear I called your phone so many times,
To feel declined,
I questioned if I was alive,
But no one see's that.

And I just keep on texting like…

                              Maybe, she didn't see that.
                                  Maybe, she's busy.
                       Maybe, she's just not interested in me.

Maybe I was the wrong one,
Adopted by the daughter,
But the mother had many problems, like I.
She had that flame in her eye.
She had,
It is not okay - to pass away – engraved in her mind,
Maybe, she finds,
What I found in the future,
But I'm a bastard,
So if I speak of dad,
I just might confuse her.

She is you.

Let me clear my throat

People think they know who I am,
At least - I think how I'm feeling,
But most of the time – I feel,
That's me just calmly pretending.

That I am - who I'm not,
That I'm good – when I'm not,
I got good at it huh?
I bet - that's why - you forgot.

I asked my uncle 'how you feelin?'
He said drop him off,
So he can ease the pain through his dealing,
I parked in front of the building
I don't mean - to be mean
And be - all in his business…
That's family,
I know,
Nobody pays him attention.

He sleep in his car,
While they sleep in a house,
He cook the food at BBQs,
And he won't sit on the couch,
He got some drank in his mouth,
Every time - I come to visit,
It's the ice cold liquor,
That picks him up off the ground.
They never understood.

He told me I'm his baby boy,
Everything is good,
He said he'll holla'
If he needs a dolla'
That wasn't a problem or nothing,
But I felt him cutting,
Himself deep - by asking from me.

Grown - talk
He understands - I'm 17,
So he vents,
And opens up the fence that I've never seen.
Don't get offensive, unc.

It was never about the green,
It's not the paper,
It's the simple fact - that someone has your back,
When you get scraped up.
And I've been scraped up,
Trying to keep my face up,
I close my eyes,
I don't see too many faces.

I'm off away to college in some months,
I'm bound for changes,
They say people just want my change ($)
But that don't really change me.

He looked angry when he told me that,
This life is crazy…
But when I listened,
I felt it phase me.
That's when I turned around and waved,
To think of all his cravings.

Just like I,
He craved love.
To I,
That was amazing.

To he,
It was the – only option.
To I,
It was another problem.
I had to opt out - He forgot bout',
The morals - which he used to know.

He guzzled – then opened up the passenger do' (door)

Started counting his dough,
He asked, what do I owe?
I said, "Enjoy yourself"
You sure? – "I'm sure"
He rattled his throat,
And said thank you…

All I did was give him a wave,
He stared empty - but thought of something simple to say,
He said,

"I love you."

Amaya

She sits there,
Eyes on gloom – shining the room,
Lighting my life,
As the high of my night.

She's growing up to be that young queen,
She always dreamed,
About being.
She left the fairytales on the street.
Touched by the way she blossomed out-
I'm very proud.

She reminds me of a butterfly,
And a wish on love's angle.

She is heaven sent,
She is one's angel.
But - she doesn't belong to me.
I belong to her.

She asked, what's wrong with me?
I couldn't even say,
She gave a simple hug,
I felt my worries decay.

I do – wish to - tell her,
Cause it's killing me.

Then, I remember,
What all of my uncles did to me.

Keep a secret,
Never illustrate you're feeling weak
"Everything's Kosher P"
Cause life isn't always sweet.

Don't hide the pain, Amaya.
You can vent to me,

I'm off to college soon,
I just hope that you remember me.

I understand that it hurts you. I love you. Be strong.

The Vent

Hope you understand,
What I'm going through.

I hope you understand,
I'm not blaming you.

I look to you and see nothing but lucid.
An illusion,
I take a step and try not to lose it.

I take a breath,
And there I go,
Trying to prove it,
I'm not stupid,
Sometimes,
I just don't - know what I'm doing.

Sometimes,
I'm blind,
I pray I find my way,
I pray I die someday,
So they - remember my smile,
While, others speak of my pain.

Youknowyouseemelookingsuicidal,
You know you see me walking round' trying to find my mind bro,
Riding the cycle.
You don't know what I've been through,
You don't see all these issues,
You're sure enough - not strong enough to peep the things on my temple,
Mentally, I'm bending back,
Physically, I'm giving back,
Spiritually, I love you, but I hate the way you used to act.

I'm a lover; not a fighter,
But I'm fighting today.

And I'm riding through the grass,
Near some dangerous snakes,

And I'm lying when I tell my mama I'm not afraid
But forward is the only way that I can get to the gates.

So let me fall forward,
At least I can afford it,
I'm broke enough,
I'm old enough to make my own mistakes,
I'm older but I'm still a chi...

Can you please wait?
You're killing me too soon,
When I'm gone,
Tell them that I - really loved you,
And you, and you,
And I hope that you believe me,
Don't defeat me,
I'm still trying to make life better for me.

Hope you understand,
What I'm going through.

Hope you understand,
When I call out for you.

To vent.

Nineteen

Ironically, the day before Valentine,
A little friend of mine,
Was born strong,
He passed not too long ago,
Oh no, here's the sad song.

Samuel Jerome Carter the third,
Entered this world,
Curled in my mother,
Pinching her nerves in 96.

I was six, I remember the very memories.
Jackie Robinson all-star,
His smile was to a - T.
He told me he would be a superstar.
And drive a fancy car,
We sagged hard,
To impress the pretty girls at Oak Park.
Smoke on mama's cigs playing hide and seek after dark
Now he's gone,
And outside is always extra dark.
I took a trip to that park,
And well…

He was on honor roll,
When it rained,
We rode our bikes to seek that pot of gold
Now he reigns high,
And when it rains - I start to shiver,
Mommy said go to bed,
And for hours we'd laugh and whisper

I remember,
He grabbed the light and burned my cheek,
I remember, he tried to drown me in the 4th feet,
I remember, he would tie the shoes on my feet,
I remember,
Those very last words he said to me.

But I won't say them.

I remember the last birthday we shared,
I remember when he blew his wishes out - I stared,
And for him,
I sit behind this sad screen and share
Erasing my tears,
He taught me to be tough.
But I don't want to be tough.

I remember when too much syrup was never enough,
On pancakes,
All the fights dad solved with belts - had us mad straight.
Laughing but mad,
Laughing but sad,
Laughing but man,

It's not so funny anymore.

I remember how he loved Kobe Bryant,
I remember sleeping on his shoulder when I was tired,
I remember, we burned a crayon,
And almost got mommy fired,
I remember the silly memories.

Early morning cartoons,
When we invented "sugar juice"
Top ramen noodles and zebra cakes,
I remember cliché
Rap songs - we would rap on – like

> *"Hey! Dirty, Baby I gotcha' money,*
> *Don't cha worry-*
> *Dirty, Baby I gotcha money"*

Now I'm worried,
Just a little.
You're still buried,
I still miss you.

I remember - how you motivate,

You are still - forever great,
I love you till the very end
RIP,
Happy Birthday – JC.

-Best friend. Brother. Love.

Red Are Roses...

Violets are blue,
Violence is truth in action,
For the angered.

I picked them while I was in the wild,
I found some later,
Next to a razor,
I scuffed mud on my Nike Blazers,
I made her a paper airplane,
That had my name - written in cursive,
I wrote it backwards on purpose,
All those little things – she encouraged,
Made my smile start curving.

I noticed,
I took notes, I focused,
I picked stones,
Watching them skip atop of rivers.
Lonely nights in December,
Remember my eve, oh spirits?

They went boom in the evening,
Oh,
You say you don't-
Know what you believe in?
I believe - you love me.

Nirvana,
You see me bungle so swift,
No Masha' Allah for I,
I find the more Socratic I get.

Nine nineteen.
She was sitting where the fine wine be.
Sweating through bliss
I can't have a kiss?
I tickled her knees.

I see illusions.
I breathe confusion,
What am I doing – here?
Somebody tell me what I'm doing, here.
These roses are red - but this life is so blue.
These voices are dead so I'm just following you.
Can you help me?

You & the Sins

Having conversations with mama,
I didn't see this coming,
I stuck the needle in you,
And that pinch interrupted.
All the things I had stuffed in,
It just spit on my comfort,
I guess you were telling me,

Suck it up Terrance – love hurts.

Conversations with gene'
He had a serious face
Instead of crying,
He thought of something simple to say…

You gon' find a buncha' girls,
And they gon' break your heart.

But on my lonesome,
I unfortunately learned that part,
I'm slowly slipping.
He slowly sipped his drink again.
I tried to see the free,
His freedom rested deep within,
His bottle – No!

What kind of life is this mama?
I'm getting tired quick mama,
I open my Bible,
Not feeling like a righteous kid, mama.
If life repeats itself,
Then why can't I recycle it, mama?
It's one love in one life,
One time to ride with this mama.
I gotta die with this mama,
I gotta hide from this mama,
Everybody got they hands out,
I don't have time for this mama.

I'm far outside with this mama,
All alone with this mama,

I'm crying,
Holding my tears back on the phone with you mama.

I keep it cool with them mama,
I be confusing them mama,
I keep my headphones in,
Cause Dajah ain't at school with me mama,
I swear,
Her and J are the only ones that's cool with me mama,
People heard lies,
I'm just thinking about the truancy mama.
Ugh.

Keep this between,
You and me mama,
28 pair of shoes - Still I feel I move empty mama.
They smile hard,
Like they got something to prove to me mama.
I turn my back,
But I still hear them whisper fluently mama.

I got my eyes open,
This rollercoaster' throwing me mama,
Under my covers is where this is controlling me, mama.
If you just walked in,
And actually asked,
"What's wrong with you?"
Maybe I wouldn't be going through,
Half the * I'm going through, mama.
Ugh.

Why you keep on ignoring me mama?
I'm not a baby,
But I need someone to court with me mama.
Where's my father?
He ain't out here on the courts with me mama,
I search for love on social media,
They feeding me mama,
I tell them eat the soup,
I just need to recoup - I got problems.

Nobody loves me (2x)

I just think it's time to be honest,
I've been modest in this game,
But who plays fair in this mama?
You missed the affairs
There's no love in the air I breathe mama
I'm breathing,
But all that means is God's preparing me mama.

My time is coming.

Lonely Rides

Cause sometimes,
I get lonely at night too,
And sometimes,
Suicide is on my mind,
I try to – not think so negative,
But who's to say what's negative?
All my close souls,
God stole,
Why can't you steal me?

I got these red Toms size 10,
So I can walk like a prince,
I keep a fantasy.

Sometimes - I put a pep in my step,
Life is too fast for me,
I stay away blasphemy
Sometimes - I feel like a young god,
Living happily
Those demons chasing after me, so.

I greet people with a smirk - or a smug
That's just - how I show love,
Even when my day - is treating me rough
I'm the type to - fall asleep on the rugs,

Singing Babylon,
It cradles my head
Like SZA & K.Dot winds,
I love winning.

Sometimes I need to be alone,
I am a sinner
Sitting searching for souls,
Someone's attacking my mirror,
And I'm blowing.

Sometimes - I feel like,

You can't speak to my mind.
I like expressing myself,
And you can't read between lines.

Therefore,
I walk on the water
Look down and drown in my comments.
To the world I'm a baby,
But to Nirvana - I got this.

To a weak mind,
I'm just another kid with a promise,
But I promise,
I got some problems,
When I'm calm - I can conquer,
I just follow my heart,
But sometimes she's afraid of the monsters.

When caution calls,
Freedom rides aren't promising pauses.

I'm riding lonely tonight,
Unless she calls,
Eager to squeeze and slowly stroke me tonight,
I only dream of being squeezed by the only,
One like,
The one they showed me, those times,
When I was down,
And needed love from a homie,
One time.

One time, she showed me her prize,
And then I lost it,
Got lost in the moment,
More for me,
More gathered profit.

More times I looked back,
Checking the ID in my wallet,
You called it,

I'm riding round' town,
But I'm lost here.

What am I doing?
What am I doing?
Oh yeah, that's right, I'm doing me.
I'm doing me.
I'm living life right now.
I just can't figure it out,
No exposure,
No exposure,
I'm lost and broken.

Catch me if you can

I've been running like Jesse Owens baby,
I ran so far away,
That you don't even know me baby.
But it's cool.

Going 92 on the freeway,
You know how teens play,
It's all fun and games,
Until you lose grip and hit the sweet pave-

I meant - to tell you it wasn't permanent,
After I caught you burning it baby,
I just figure,
That both of us don't deserve this,
Maybe?

We can try aga-
Nope! I'm tired of trying this baby,
I've been running away from home,
I lost my mind again – lately.

I just been contemplating.
Cocking my bb,
And going bang – it gets complicated.
Novacane, sing it Frank,
Turn down the conversations,
Don't mute the music.
I know you don't get me,
That's pretty - it's actually beauty.
It actually threw me around the corner, eluting.
Let's change the subject.

I was walking and saw a mother,
Like 19,
I thought of you and said,
Look at her, that can be *she*,
I looked at her baby boy,
And said - that could be me.

But you don't get it. Nah, you just don't get it.

Condoms on the street,
That's the scenery,
You and the sins,
Depicted in the same picture,
I picture that kid.

I'm living baby,
On the other side of the hills,
I have a vision baby,
But when I'm down – I'm ugly.
And when I get the things that I've been dreaming for,
It's lovely.

I'm running to find life,
Don't hug, kiss me, or touch me.
If I'm running,
How can you be rooting for me?
If you're loving me?
When loving me is slowing me down,
If you keep loving me,
Then how will I learn to love myself?

I – love – myself,
I heard Kendrick singing,
I wish I believed him,
He probably said it,
Cause someone said,
Don't show them your weakness.

***** *- don't - kill - my - vibe.*
That's that line that's retrieving,
When I hear those violins,
I feel my worries decreasing.

But when you kill my vibe,
Everything starts to increase,
You told me not to lie,
Truth is, my truth isn't sweet

My truth is bitterness – the * that makes your heart bleed,
I told you don't believe,
In every little thing that you see.

This life is crazy baby,
Just think of it as - me going on a vacation baby,
These mental stages got me wrapped up,
I'm tangled baby.
I'm in the game,
Just say my name,
Cause I can't fake it,
If the real feels too strange.

This life is crazy baby,
Same ones that's in your face,
Want to kill you,
If you're a part of me - they try to steal you.

I dropped my knife a long time ago,
And started running,
Cause I'd hate to see my white T – start to get bloody.

I'm out here running like Jesse Owens,
I owe you nothing.
I love in person,
But my love hurts,
So through my poems - I do my cursing.
I don't wish to hurt you.

Just trynna tell you the truth.
Tell the world,
So - they can see the stem of my roots.
The little root of evil - killing people,
Sent me to you,
So I just turned my life around and started making some moves
Don't be confused,

You know where I be. Don't be sad. Reach for my hand. I'll be running. Catch me, if you can.

Part Ten: Pretty Foreign

Philia

Eros

Agape

Storge

Philia (Brotherly Love)

The Greek word Philia can be often translated as "brotherly love". For as long as I can remember, brotherly love has always been present in my life. I was born second to last out of my two brothers and one sister. I experienced Philia all throughout my childhood.

I found Philia on rainy days outside getting soaked in the rain with my big brother and all of our friends. Philia was on the basketball courts and skating rinks. Every day my brother and I would get home from school, do our homework, and then ask our sister, "Can we go outside?"

About 10 of us, all friends, would make our way down to the basketball court or skating ring to go play. If we weren't enjoying our youth at the courts or rolling on skates, we were playing marbles, street hockey, or just hanging around eating snacks and getting dirty on the playgrounds across our complex.

In Southeast of San Diego, all the kids I grew up with had very similar lives. It was either they had both parents in their household making it work, one parent in their house while the other is dead or in jail, or both parents in the house on drugs somehow making the ends meet. The big boys on the corner were selling drugs, and even when I was about six years old I knew that.

Some of my friends had parents that didn't show too much concern for where their children were or what their children were doing. My sister and mother always told my brother and I, if we say we're going somewhere, we better be there, because if they went calling for us and we weren't where we said we would be, there was going to be some problems. My friends would stay outside until dark sometimes and nothing would happen to them. In my household, my brothers and I always had a curfew.

My greatest memories of Philia were from 2000-2004, back before my brother Samuel passed away. When he passed away, I no longer felt like I had Philia inside of me anymore. I felt all alone. I had lost my brother physically at the age of 7, and losing him was the hardest obstacle of my life.

As life continued, I learned to create brotherly bonds with the guys in the new neighborhoods I would bounce around to. I moved from my household when my brother passed away and my life was never the same. I had to make new friends when I switched schools. In that first year, I met some of my best friends that I still keep in contact with.

There was one person that followed me in my life and his name is Curtis Hampton. Curtis was in my life when my brother was alive. I remember we would sometimes go to the skating rink or just roam around the complex getting into trouble. Having Curtis as a friend from elementary school until now has always been an eye-opener for me. He reminds me daily of the importance of brotherly love. Every time we get the chance to hang out and reminisce on life, we both share stories about how far back we go. And as life moved fast for me, I still continued to mourn from the loss of my blood brother. With that being said, I grew a strong love for all of my guy friends.

There was another one of my friends, now that I call my brother, Jordan Bell. Jordan and I met in middle school around the third quarter of my sixth grade year. Dude was one of the fastest kids at my school and he proved that in his first week of attendance. From the first day that I saw him in P.E running that fast we have been cool. Jordan and I are still best friends today. His mother looked at me as if I were one of her children. And my mother, shares the same love towards him. Our stage of Philia grew back in middle school. We can always look back and talk about how life used to be. When I look at Jordan, or walk in his house, watch some basketball or a comedy show, and just sit and talk about the tragedies of our modern day lives; I notice the growth in the both of us. I can tell myself that I have a brother who is always there for me. He's always there for me no matter if I am feeling up or down.

That's the true definition of a brother. Though we are two different kids with two different backgrounds, we complete one another. Without him in my life, I feel that I would have no competition. Just like a little brother to a big brother, there's something in the little brother's heart that pushes him to want to be better than or impress his big brother. Without Jordan in my life, I'm not sure how far I'd be along writing this book. For he was one of my biggest supporters who always told me to keep pushing myself and rising above to be a leader and a role model.

I have a little brother named Desmond. We call him "Des" in my family. Our Philia was the most memorable to me before he got into his teenage years. Back in the day, he would want to do everything with me. If I went to the playground or the liquor store, he wanted to go too. If I was playing the game, he wanted to play the game. If I wanted some juice, he wanted some juice too. I was the person that he always wanted to be around because he was so attached to the love shared between us.

He knew that he could lay on me and run around the house and play little games. He would make me humble myself so that he could find his true happiness. He found it within me. Des would nag "Let me shoot it!" when we played basketball. I would always go extra hard on him. Sometimes, so hard that he would cry and give up. I would make him feel so low about himself that he wasn't strong, so that he could **want** to be **successful**. I would always tell him, "You'll never be on the television like Kobe, or like Michael Jordan if you quit." And he would say, "So what? I'm young. I don't have to be like them, yet." I was never trying to destroy him and truly kill his confidence, I was just trying to show him that he had to work hard to get the things that he wanted in life. These days were when he was about five through eleven.

Once Des became a teenager I let my hands off of him so that he could grow. I left him alone in his room when he wanted to be. Sometimes, when I would come home from school, I'd only say "Hey, what's up?" and walk straight into my room. We even shared a room for a couple of years and the only time we talked was if a sports game was on or if we were going outside to play football.

When he would eat this food, he would grab a cereal box or some junk mail on the dinner table and cover his face with it. He did not enjoy when I would look at him while he was eating food. I don't know why he acted this way towards me; I just know that without a doubt that was his way of showing love. He never really had to say "I love you" to make me feel that he was close to me. There was a feeling that he gave me without trying to. This love was unconditional. We didn't have to say any words to each other all day sometimes, but I knew when we made eye contact or a football game came on, that our brotherly love would be felt in those hours.

My little brother taught me that love isn't always spoken in language or through affection. Love is something that follows more of what you do than what you say.

Eros (Sexual desire and attraction)

This type of love was a love that I had to find out what it meant to me all on my own. My parents stayed away from teaching me this one. How did I learn this? I learned about this Greek god of sexual desire and attraction by becoming attracted to lust. I believe that a growing young man, with all the stress in his life, more easily becomes connected with this part of his mind.

Visiting this stage of love, can be good and bad. In Christianity, God tells his children to not have any sex until marriage. As a kid, I used to think of sex a lot. A lot more than I should have been thinking of it. I don't know why it grew on me so early. Maybe it was because I always felt that I could never escape from it. I mean, the effect of this sexual desire and attraction is a huge reason to why I am breathing right now. I guess with my father's lessons on my mind at a very young age, sex was something that almost never left my mind as I grew into the young man that I am today.

Love is such a beautiful thing. There is nothing wrong with lust. Say, it is what drives two people to create beautiful experiments and memories. There is nothing wrong with "dreaming" of someone as long as you know your limits. God wants his children to be wise about their decisions. You know what I'm talking about. But as far as your desires, you just have to take the time to learn when the right time in life it is to use them. Love is something beautiful and appealing to the eye by all means; but if we use it the wrong way, then our results are expected to make love seem very ugly.

I have a sister named Dashanna, but everyone calls her "Shonnie". My sister is my heartbeat. When I was younger, I never realized how much she bent her back to watch over me. She always made sure that I was safe, as well as my other two brothers. I'll speak on my behalf when I tell this story about her but, she was always in my ear playing too grown or too protective. It's almost as if I was her son the way that she took care of me when my father passed away and my mother was on drugs.

Every time I needed something she would go out of her way to get it for me. And I mean, by any means.

My sister taught me the basics about love in a relationship or even just in family. She would always say, "As long as love is love; it is what it is," which was one of my grandmothers' favorite quotes.

Shonnie had a rough childhood. Growing up being bounced around from household to household I guess I can let you imagine the kind of life she had. I guess that's why when I was young and she saw me going through tough times she was there to support mentally. She had already been through the fire so she tried her hardest to pull me out with all of her strength.

Sometimes my cousins came over to our house to kick it and watch movies. Sometimes they had friends outside who would kick it, smoking blunts and enjoying their youth. My sister kept me away from those people. Even though I said my "what's up" to them and they knew me as "little dude" I still kept my distance when they would be near my house. My sister had to be my guardian at all times. She is the example of (my brother's keeper).

One thing that my sister always made me do was cover my eyes when we watched a movie that had a sex scene come up. It would get really quiet. She'd tell me "Stop trynna peek; you ain't slick" I'd have to hide my face behind a pillow but I still focused hard on what was going on. I'd listen ten times harder just so that I can use my imagination to see what was so bad about me watching a sex scene at a young age. As a young child lust had my attention. That's about all that I knew when my mother was absent in my life.

Just like my mother always taught me, "Everything that you hide from me, is what's going to mess up your life." Not to down my sister, but she had her first child at 15. We all know that's a rough situation to be in when you are still legally a "child". I can see why my sister and mother always told me to stay away from sex. It can mess up your life, body, and focus. I've seen my peers end up having sex and creating families early on and I've learned that life is not fit for me.

My mother raised me to not have sex before marriage. As this is what my family has practiced since I was born. Was it always like that? No. Did people in my family fall short? Yes. But the simple fact that my mother taught me to wait for sex is the forceful thought that always kept me away from getting involved with it. I am a teenager and lust does travel my way it seems almost a hundred times a day. But with the focus that God has given me added onto the teachings that my mother has taught me, I am devoted to practice such a lifestyle.

My sister, Shonnie, is one of my biggest supporters. I love her dearly and my life wouldn't be nowhere near the same had she not been present in my life.

Agape

The Modern Greek word, "Agape" can be translated in words such as, compassion, forgiveness, charity; the love of God for man and of man for God.

This type of love is an everlasting love. Nobody on this Earth can give you Agape love except God. His love is forever. God promises his children that he will never leave or forsake them. One of the biggest differences between Gods love and the love that is of the Earth is, God's love doesn't change. Love of the Earth is deceiving and shaky. One day "love" can be a joyful ride and on other days it can take you on the worst ride of your life.

Agape love cannot change. Agape is one way all the time. While other types of love feed your mentality; Agape love feeds your spirit, mind, body, and soul.

An example of my Agape love from God would be all of the messages that He gives me to write about. Without God's love I wouldn't be where I am today. Mentally, my mind wouldn't have the strength to believe in something of a higher power controlling the world that circles around me. Agape love never fails. It is what wakes us up every morning to renew our plates of yesterday. Agape love is given to us daily by God himself.

We need this love from God because it allows us to recognize what true love is. When you feel this love as it is present in your life, you soak in every bit of it. God will overflow your cup. He will "make sure you're straight." He will dip your soul in His love and shower you with His blessings.

God is amazing. He is love.

Storge

Pinpoint the moment,
Hormones exploded,
We were devoted,
And easily,
Swung in the motion, okay?

I'll get you,
But then I'm searching for more.
I'm with you,
Break this predictable bore.

Loving you is complicated,
We painted our patience,
Praying for pages,
Embracing changes,
Changing ways, we paranoid?

Exceptional lovers loving,
Stomach kisses in public,
Held pinkies,
Slow quickies,
I know you need me.

Touching what can't be felt,
By oneself,
I understand that you need some help.

I'll help you,
Help me,
Help you,
Burn with the birds,
And sleep with the bees.
Get it? Ha.

Just friends?
When can we even fake it?
We can't,
But we squeeze til it feels complacent.

I decided that one day,
You should come,
Looking for my body.
Probably.

Part Eleven: A Spruced Philosophy

Burning Passion

Burdens

Adrenaline Rush

The Past

His Beauty

He Doesn't Know

Opposites (Man & Woman)

Love is "I"

CC's Poem

Baby, Don't Sleep

Fall for you

Along Came a Spider

A Book to a Brain

It Ain't Easy

Her Roses

Dive

The Last Spruce Standing

The Good Kids' Dream

Burning Passion

There's something inside of us all,
Pushing us to be greater.
Saying give a compliment to a stranger,
Give one a hug for a little longer than usual,
This person, tells us to stay calm in hectic times,
And pushes the poison out of our lives,
As long as we let it work and do its job.

We must listen to that voice inside of us daily.

There is a present that God gave us all,
That present is us being present.
We need to be thankful for our gifts.
We shall not be greedy with what God blesses us with,
We must learn to be humble and give to others,
We must teach others the way of proceeding in progress.
We must do for others so that one day others will do unto us.
We must complete another's cipher to become complete.
We must know that no human is of more value than another.
We must spread love each day we are granted.

In order to lead someone,
You have to take the initiative to lead yourself.
If you cannot find that burning passion within yourself to lead
others,
You must grow to find it.
For it is not what we do for ourselves,
But what we do for others that makes our lives of any value.
Lead young one,
Lead old soul,
My world, this world, our world, needs you.

Our actions are mere expressions of our inward voices.
Stay connected with your inner voice.
Study and grow from it,
For this will help you develop into a better individual.
Get connected.

It will take you many places on this Earth and enrich your mind, body, and soul.

Love is not an abstract thing,
Loving yourself is not a sign of danger
You are no threat to anyone but yourself (who lacks self-love)
You are the courage.
Push, listen to that voice, and grow.

Burdens

Sometimes things just sneak up on you.
Old pains from the past always come after you,
When you seem to finally start doing well.

Right when you get comfortable, boom.
There they come.

Every day make it a challenge to add positives in your life.
The more positive things you walk towards and collect,
The less amount of burdens you hold.

The key to a happy life,
Is having the drive to collect as many positive gifts as possible.

Those who collect negatives gain more burdens.
Some people love to keep burdens on them,
Those people tend to be the ones who always complain,
Cry, want handouts, and stay in drama.

The best thing to do when you are holding burdens is to try to be
grateful for all of the positive gifts that you have. Even if you only
have **one** thing to be grateful for in the moment. Be grateful for it.

Always remember,
Somebody out there,
Very close or far away,
Is living a life that it worse than yours.
Somebody has it worse.

Drop your burdens and ask God to take them off of your shoulders.
He will slowly start to take care of your burdens as you-
Keep your eyes and faith on him to take care of you.

Stack your positives,
Like old rich men stack their chump change.

For one day,
You,

Just like them,
Will be rich.

Not necessarily rich as in wealth,
But surely rich in spirit.

Adrenaline Rush

We just need to slow the speed,
93 MPH,
The vibes are so bitter-

I see you shiver, geez.
I see you look at me,
Visualizing the crashes,
On the 94 East.

We're one step away,
And only one breath away.
We're set so far back,
We're still living in yesterday.

You give me a little rush,
By kissing me with the look,
That looks inside of my lust,
For beliefs,
We don't feed on luck.

We're just moving too fast,
You don't see me,
But I see you,
Removing your mask.

I know you're scared,
And with life you're searching for your affair,
You roll the windows up,
You cannot bear the air.

We don't care,
Young rebels with settlements,
The further we both travel,
The slicker the devil gets.

And oh how he pushes us,
To dive into this love,
We trust in his trick words,

But in the end – it's fun.

What are we sposed' to do?
You say enjoy the youth,
God said be healthy,
So, yes we ate the fruit.

Just how the devil wanted,
Healthiness he had flaunted,
Better live he had taunted,
And all the things we hid,
Soon or later,
Came back and haunted.

So maybe we need to watch the speed limit,
We're just rushing,
For solutions we aren't getting,
Walking in soles that we surely aren't fitting,
Our pictures on Instagram,
Make it all look appealing.

But they don't feel us crashing-
Laughing and bashing our heads.
They just tell us we look good,
Are they our friends?

Do they pretend?
Are they too feeling the rush?
They must be,
If they really think we are in love.

Don't rush this life. Don't rush anything. You cannot control everything. Daily I ask God, is this really love that I'm feeling? He proves to me what true love is when he blesses me. I am breathing. I am living. Stop trying to control everything. Stop trying to control the way the world spins. God handles all of that. It is his job to take care of the world. Recognize His power. Recognize that He is greater than you, and any and everything else in this world. When you give him the recognition He deserves; He will give you the desires of your heart.

Chill with your adrenaline rush. Relax and take a deep breath. Life is supposed to be something you enjoy; not something that you destroy. Let God take care of you.

The Past

The past is the past; leave it there.
You can't even get close to growth,
If you chose to remain stagnant in yesterday's adventures,
Happiness, and pain.

Yesterday is a memory that is irreplaceable.
The only thing you can do about yesterday is live,
With a drive to make today and tomorrow better for yourself,
And everyone else around you.

The past can either do two things:
It can build you; or destroy you.

Some people use their past as motivation,
To push themselves.

Other people use their past as a lock,
A lock that locks their past and stays connected to them,
In the present tense.
In other words, some never let go of their past.
They let it hold them back,
They use their old pains and trials,
As an excuse of why they can never move on.

Well listen here dude,
Everyone has a past.
Everyone has been through something.
And I know it sounds pretty harsh,
But 'Suck it up and get through it.'

If you're still locked to your past,
To the point where you can't even move on,
You have a problem.

It can take years and years to learn how to let go.
But eventually, one day you have to,
Before it's too late.

Life is too short,
Hold the past in your heart; forget the past in your mind.

God's present to us is for us to be present.
The future isn't promised.
Live now. Live today. Live.

His Beauty

Everything was already written.
So beautiful and intricate.
Life is full of choices.

It's all on you.
You have to hop on that path of enlightenment.
You have to know your true potential,
And even harder, believe in it.

We're so scared to find our true selves,
We protect ourselves so much from ourselves,
That we don't even know who we really are.

We spend our whole lives,
Inside of our own shell but trying to fit into a mask,
That will be comfortable for others to see us as.

Do we really know how we see ourselves?
Not by staring into a mirror,
But by releasing what makes us feel inferior?

We are bigger than what we appear to be,
Even though our life is as fragile as a balloon.
Our lives are still great tanks of joy.

A joy that is found within.
A joy that derives from only God's love.

From this worldly love,
You don't get everything that you want.
You are failed many times.
When you don't get what you hope for,
You change mentally.
Your attitude can flip very easily.
Your personality can be destroyed.
Your sense of hope can fade.
An upset in love can make you change.

Love, can make you do some crazy-
But maybe because that's not true love.

There is a love that is better.
A love that can never bend nor break.
That is the love that you find within,
Yourself; not in others.

He Doesn't Know

He doesn't know love,
Until they teach it to him.

He doesn't know kiss,
Until he has seen them do it.

He doesn't know pain,
Matter of fact, yes he does.

But he knows redemption,
Before he knows to give up.

He doesn't know you,
Until you have said Hello.

He doesn't know the truth,
Until the lies make him grow.

He knew of no style,
Until his people grooved.

He didn't know accomplishment,
But you've seen him lose.

He doesn't know – that you know,
That you don't know what you say.

And he guesses,
He's just living off of what you portray.

He knows no life,
He knows all sin.
He knows that he should've just looked within.

To find the answers.

Opposites (Man & Woman)

I am man,
I am man in universe.
I am closest to woman,
The woman looks.

I am woman,
I am woman in galaxy.
I am closest to man,
The man is shook, without me.

I am man,
From the soil, to the blood that boils,
I am lung,
And she, is me, after ribs.

I am woman,
From the rib, to the breast,
I am intellect,
And he, is my, footstep.

I am man,
Second nature, from God,
In the breeze I am strength,
In the calm, I am none,
From the palm, I create.

I am woman,
Third nature,
From the tree I consumed
In my name, you inherit pain,
As it haunts you.

I am man,
Of sin, too. I fall like leaves,
I am quick with haughty eyes,
And apologies.

I am woman,
I am what the Second wanted,

In the seconds of conscience,
I'm the pudding of the problem.

I am man,
In the seconds, I have wanted, you.
Crawling down my collar, you.
Tell me eat the fruit.
Before the truth swallow you.

I am woman, and I lie.
I have many battle wounds,
You don't see the lower case,
You are my capital.

I am man, cannon boom.
Heartbroken and confused,
Down to groove in the music,
But the winds make me move.

I am woman, I am willing
To sin with you,
If you promise,
Me a lifetime ride - in the blues.

I-I-I love you.

Love is "i"

"Terrance, what is love?"

Love is you.
Love is her.
Love is him.
Love is God.
Love is "i"

Love, is-
The very first step walking out of the door,
Smiling at the greenery and floating in the fresh winds.

Love, is-
Paying attention and learning.
Love is a joyful smile on the inside.
Love is quiet.
But sometimes it can be very loud.

Love, is "i"
Love is discipline.
Love is hugging thy neighbor.
Love is a warm greeting.
Love is faithful.
Love is loyal.
Love is never ending, unconditional, and complete.

Love is easy.
But sometimes it can be hard.
Love is light,
Just some days, it can be dark.

Love is a soft finger slide under a chin, and a fragile kiss on the
forehead.
Love is responding rather than reacting.
Love is calm.
Love is very patient.
But sometimes it can hit you a little too hard.

Love has no time.
Love is always.
Love is saying "no" when your mind tells you "yes"
Love is being the bigger person.
Love is under no control.

Love is you.
Love is her.
Love is him.
Love is God.
Love is "i"

I, as in,
I am what love is,
I represent love,
God's love toward his children.

If we are made in his image,
Then we must be a piece of who He is.
He says that He made us in his image.
Only not of His power.

And if God is full of love,
Then so am I - and so are you, too.

So why do we scream, riot and build hatred my sister?
Put that gun down my brother.
You must not kill another to destroy our mothers.

We are all the same piece of the pie,
We are just cut into our own sizes.
We may all "look" different.
But in our minds, we can one day learn to see,
That on the inside,
No matter what differences we have on the outside,
That we are all made the same.
We are the human bodies,
All made exactly the same way.

Love is "I"

Because 2/2 = 1.
We are all made in God's image. God is love.
Think of God as one big ocean.
We are all made from God.

If you divide any number by itself,
It will equal 1.
Though, we are plural, we are all the same.
Individually, we are 2,3,4,5, and 6…
But when you divide us as individuals,
We then become 1.
"I" is 1.
Two eyes - one vision – one love.

CC's Poem

It's not what's right in front of you.
Face reality - stop imagining.

You make the best out of all situations, yes.
But not so much that you let a burden continue to stay concrete in
your life.

You can't hate someone until you really love them.
There's a thin line between love and hate.

You told me,
Failure is my forte,
And love can be my fortune,
But unfortunately,
We don't think it's important,
To go by the rules.

Do I love you because I need you?

Do I need you because I love you?
And can't stop thinking of you?

Beach dates, the sun just beams,
Over your features,
Featuring my lips,
We don't like being facetious.

We gave everyone our "everything"
What else do we have to give?
What else are we searching for?
We don't even want to live.

Sometimes, all we learn to do,
Is learn and sin,
And pray in silence,
Hoping that He still forgives.

For my CC,

Cover my questions with a kiss,
This is for all of the letters you've sent me.
All the teachings,
All the lessons,
All of our love sessions,

Thank you for teaching me.

Baby, Don't Sleep

When she starts gripping her pillow - drifting to sleep....
I start gripping my pencil to drift oh so deep...

I come alive right now,
I come alive right now!
I'm in disguise,
There's no more cherry in my pie, right now.
Meaning in life, there's only one place to hide right now.

Behind my feelings,
Feeling you,
Feel how I die, cry now?

Don't sleep.

I saw you sitting there, in silence.
Your sitting, kind of reminded, me.
Kicking it turns to kids, being grown, but still kids.
And when, it all falls down, you just grin, again.

Little friend, I saw you.
Looking through the pensive kiss,
Pending at the passenger.
Passing you past the bitterness.
It could be so simple, you know.
I know – you love living big

I can tell you love dreaming,
And dreaming can bring you sickness,
Sinning in all honesty to find forgiveness in fabrication,
I saw you being creative,
I saw you – relating,
To devastative conversation.
Complex and complicated,
Compressed feelings – in your converse

I swerve in my concerns, as I crossed too.
I was just sitting there dreaming,
To pass by you.
To tell you a little story about love, in silence.

Fall For You

You have to fall in love with yourself,
Without the help of another.
Without the help of a helper in hell who dwells in a substance.
Without your guardian who's guarding you from golden gates of solitude.
Fall in love so deep with yourself - egos cannot bother you.

Be expressive,
Spend time in harmony,
Harmonize with a swarm of bees,
Until you're stuck,
Loving yourself,
Scratch the anatomy,
The masterpiece is an eye closed,
With the potential to split an ego into an idol.

May your enemies be the ones you love the most.
May your inner peace be found outside of bowls.
May accomplishments be made from light stones,
That hit Goliath, and killed a giant, with a wise dome.

How about we practice progression?
Because the numb souls,
Numbed every number,
And I lost, connections.

My old friends,
Turned cold, like coast winds,
Complexity simplified,
Drove my soul near a whoa-spin,
Now my soul has been spinning,
Now my loving side, is noticed.
I'm more excited with leaning,
In lessons, to cause something explosive.

I really just want to BE free, and the road is yet, before me.
I never saw the clear road,
Until I wrote,
My own story.
I am love.

Along Came a Spider

You ever see a spider try to climb up from the floor surface to the side wall? It struggles trying to get up because some of its legs are on the floor surface and he has to switch his balance and shift towards the side wall. In the spiders' process, it has to repetitively keep working to get onto the wall. If you ever watch a spider do this, you'll either want to help the spider get to the side wall and continue its climb, or watch it continue to fall, and if you're a jerk, kill it.

In life, we are that spider. We reach for love and certain things in life and continue to fall. We know that we fall, but we choose to keep trying things the same way. Just like the spider, we have to find and use different alternatives for us to get up our walls in life.

Love comes with trials and tribulations. You will never find true love without figuring out what it feels like to be in Magic Land. A voice in your head will tell you to be prideful, forget what people say, it's all about you and what you want. Having that ego in love, is the first step to entering Magic Land. You have to listen to the voice in your head that tells you to walk the other way, and not go searching for love.

Your natural true voice talks to you, it tells you to stop, look and listen. Stop trying to climb the wall like the spider that continues to fall on its back. Take a moment, look within, love is right there. Deep down in the middle of your soul, close your eyes and you will feel it moving inside of you. A burning joy that moves you like nothing else in this life can. It is the spirit, the free and clean spirit. There it is, love. Boiling inside of you, love. Patiently waiting for you to accept it and live with it genuinely, love.

When the ego of that spider dies,
It finals begins to live.

Lose your ego.
Find yourself,
Find love.

A Book to a Brain

I was talking to a female in my math class and she told me,

"It's dangerous to believe in something that doesn't change."

A weak mind can't handle that.

She asked me, "What's a book to a brain?"

Words written in a book are frozen. The words can't move. The words can't explain themselves furthermore. But you, have the ability to go above and beyond with what you "understand."

You can understand something so much that you no longer "understand" it, you just learn to accept it for what it is.

We have the power to change our minds at any second.
Our brains are powerful enough to move.
Words that are locked inside of books no longer move.

Words have the power to move a mindset,
That's why authors continue to write more and more.
You can't change what has already been written and set in place.

We have to learn to accept the things that we cannot change and focus on moving our minds so that we can change the way we think.

Too many of us want direct answers.

It's those people who don't use their time wisely by not reading, observing with others, or becoming one with themselves, that miss out on understanding love.

I wish I could teach everyone about love,
I statistically cannot do that. (At least not all by myself)

What's a book to a brain? A brain can learn something new every second of the day.

A book, is a tool that we use to exercise our minds to know more. The frozen words inside of a book do not move, nor change their place. The only thing that a human brain can do when reading a book, is read the book the way it is simply written, or change their view of the words and make personal connections with the words written. As humans, our brains have so much power that we are unaware of because we spend too much time not using our brains to their fullest potential. When we take the time to sit down and read a book we are exercising our mind. We have the power to be as thoughtful and elusive in our minds as we want to. Once a book is complete, not you or even the author can change the meaning behind the words inside. They mean exactly what they mean.

A word cannot grow from you reading it, but a word can make you grow. Think about it. What the girl was stressing was that just knowing that simple fact is scary but beautiful.

When you know just how much your mind can consume and receive, you are more willing to feed it more. You cannot feed a book more words; but a book can feed you plenty. Get it?

It Ain't Easy

I never parked on this side of the street.
9 words that hurt my mind more than,
Rain hurt mother's spine.
More than, strains straining my decline through my recliner.

I'm on the other side of the street,
It feels so good right here.
It feels so hood right here.
My hood squeezing my thoughts,
It's Trayvon right here.

Admitting is the first step,
The rain is suicidal and it's coming for its attempt.
I'm pretty content with that one step,
Til I two step, in a new dress,
Then that's new stress,
Then the rain stops.

And when the rain stops-
The pain hops,
From intermediate to expert.

Keys to the right and I'm swerving,
Life? I never deserved this.
You're right. I don't be need to be nervous.
I'm doing,
Who said I wanted to prosper?
Prosperity in my past,
I'm gon' need some water.

I've never parked on this side of the street,
But the rain told me to listen,
To my blessings and to know that I'm forgiven,
Yes, I'm the sinner,
Who will one day commit once more,

Until I fall like Samuel,
In the middle of the floor,

Holding my heart.

I never followed his footsteps,
Though I knew how to find,
His legacy,
Then, I made up my mind.

Her Roses

I throw away the dying flowers,
I no longer sit with scents on the couches.

I drained the water from the clear vase,
On her face was a student,
Confused and ready to lose it,
I had to do it; it stunk up the place.

I took a sip of the poison,
Just to see how it tastes,
Honestly, I was curious,
To see what we've made.

Out of the ashes,
I'm thinking out loud,
I walk through the field,
Hearing the crowds.

Dear God,
You stationed me way too close to these clouds.

I don't want roses.
They look beautiful,
But soon they die.
And I don't want to see myself die.

Those Nineteen roses,
Meant love was waiting for me,
You were thinking of you,
And I was thinking of spring.

Autumn was lovely,
But April's looking for me.
And I told them both,
Don't give me nothing to make me sneeze.

I just want what's full of purity,
Something maturity lends.

Something that's heaven sent,
Something good for my sins,
To slip away.

Baby, I won't need none of your roses today.

I am my own rose.

Dive

Have you ever dove into Leviticus?
Numbers, did you dig in Deuteronomy,
Did you drown in the message?
Who are you following?

Probably
Pushing sins before a psalm,
In your palm,
Passing points in Proverbs to pause.

Pushing flaws so far away,
Pointing fingers pinning problems of today,
Promising peace in numb love,
Who are you following?

Cross the blood on the cross,
Is that the same love washing sins?

Glorify the weaker mind,
That's just how the devil slides,
Lucy in a pair of Gucci sneakers,
Who's she sneaking too?

Love is from the one,
That comes and sums the dumb between the two,
She is art,
She is the universe I'm ripping apart.
With my two fingers.

I write about her,
History, past, present,
Not future, because we knew,
In a matter of seconds,
We would be the ones to be tested,
We knew the struggles of that love commitment.

And that commitment,
Uh well, we weren't really with it.

She was into sneaking,
Away from everything she needed,
And I was into believing,
Things happened for a reason.

The more she dreamt; the more down I would get.

The Last Spruce Standing

*I picked up my head from a pile of soft leaves matted together
forming a fluffy pillow. All night long I was slow dancing by myself
and dreaming of having someone to dance with. I pushed away from
the dry soil I had been resting in. Onto my feet, I stood to stop and
stare at the beauty in my presence. It felt as if I were still dreaming.
In both physical and mental states, I began to travel. Ahead of me
was a narrow path. Close up I could see everything.*

*As life was distant from my eyesight, nature appeared to be sought in
blurs. I wasn't blind to the snakes slithering in a slow motion near
the thorns in the garden to the left of me. The branches on the trees
on both sides of this narrow path whispered a chilly melody. A soft
echo from the winds' voice trapped me inside of my own stage of
understanding. I understood my fears but held onto my courage to
block my nearest thoughts of giving up. I had a goal. A goal worth
achieving so much that I would do just about anything to get it
accomplished. I remembered having a conversation with a man...*

I finally opened my eyes. Guess who I came across? That same man
meditating next to a stack of newspapers and a box of peaches and
grapevines. He stopped in the middle of meditation and the both of
us made eye contact. I said a silent prayer, and took a step towards
him with no fear at all. He grabbed a waist bag, stood up, and gave it
to me. He saw the mystery in my eyes. I saw the answers in his. And
with his eyes locked firmly onto my soul, he told me, "I don't mean
to scare you. How's it going?"

I said, "I'm living."
"Well, are you?"

"Look sir, not to be in your business,
But how are you living here in a tent with an intention to judge?"

"How are you living in this day - still searching for love?
How do you stare me in the face and feel compelled to judge?
Who do you think you are?
You're like the lady who passed by,
I gave her this bag for the times, she gets lost,

Falls off, and wants to feel alive.
She wanted to be comfortable by looking for a light.
I'm convinced that's the truth.
And she was, looking for the love - by searching through you?

"Yes."

"Perhaps you do not know love. No matter how smart you get. Love can take you years to know. Yes, you are intelligent. But she cannot tell that you – don't know of love, and that's why she's hooked as if love was a sick drug. Love – is – patient."

"Love is creation and we focused on creating something that the world created."

"Yes. Love is creative. So create your own pages. Learn to spell it out with your own pen and paper."

"You're telling me that - if I just illustrate an image,
I'll no longer take these mental visits?
And Sasha, who loves to dream - will soon visit me?

"Write it out righteous - and tell me what you see, eventually."

"But what about the motions of the way I move my hand?"

"Fail and succeed and you'll find it soon, man."

"Well, where do I start off? I don't know what to write."

"Write about the false love trips of your life."

"And then I'll know?..."

> *"And then you'll know the power of your hands,*
> *And chose to lose the poison,*
> *That you sip in Magic Land"*

That wise man told me, "Go! Go find it"

But I had to write my last letter to Sasha…

The Good Kids' Dream

Just continue being strong for me.
And if you're falling,
Continue to keep our lows low-key.

Make sure that when you speak of Rosie, Sasha comes to mind, and
doesn't mind to hold me.

I don't need all the controversy,
It's been too complicated,
I'm still crossing the path that crosses her narrow journey.

I told you I wasn't there,
But now I'm here,
I was in my feelings too long,
Your state of conscience disappeared.

Remember when we were just friends?
And just a simple smile turned to a grin?
Your riddles rested,
I didn't know that the joke was resting in my bed.

I told you that you were sleeping,
Sophisticated and reaching,
For reasons to hold me back,
It was you, who did all the screaming.

I was just in my bed, sinking to misery.
Touching you and loving you,
For chemistry and sympathy.

You can say that I loved you,
Using your gift for my pleasure,
Wipe away all the pain,
I sat you on top of the dresser,
We cuddled in all this whether, remember you said you love?
It - how we dipped,
How we sinned and you were my sensation?

I was saving myself,
Just to give you the glory.
What is your perspective, huh?
This is - my story!

Yes, I am a Good Kid,
That's what they all think.
They thought we looked good,
They thought it was your dream.

They thought that I promised,
And learned to give the best love.
But I didn't love myself,
So yes - I messed up.

And yes I left you,
Yes, I walked away.
I never came back,
Yes, that was child's play.

Yes, it was heart felt,
Yes, I really felt,
Feeling you,
Was way better - than being all by myself.

Should've never left you,
Should've stayed where I dwelled,
I should've called 911,
You said you'd die if I'd tell?

Now, you're still sleeping,
Please, come out the shell,
Remember me?
We were - once a fairytale.

Can I tell the story now?
Can I really tell them how?
Love is something,
That - in myself - I've found.

I did it to you,
You did it to me,
We sipped the poison,
And the good,
Was so bittersweet.

Now, I'm just starting deep,
Watching you sleep away,
Stuck in this Magic Land,
Why do you want to stay?

If we did it well enough,
We both shouldn't want it more.
I remember walking in,
Just as you closed the door.

They say you hung yourself,
You couldn't take the pain.
Now everybody says they miss you,
When I say your name.

I try to be the rose, Rosie.
The rose you taught me to be.
But I die every time,
I hear the songs that we'd sing.

I told you I'll never leave,
I'll stay till infinity,
But infinity dies,
If the trinity is incomplete.

If we do not know God,
We do not know we,
I do not know you,
And you do not know me.

I didn't even love myself,
Young in love - loving you,
Unlucky, I never found it,
And that's why I'm leaving you.

I have to find myself.
To know myself.
And love myself.

Sasha, when you awake,
I promise to help.

But if I die, before you wake,
I promise that I'll never eat from the same plate,
As you, I look at you and go,
Should've listened to mama,
She told me so.

Oh she told me - about the poison.
She said it can kill,
And I sit here, waiting for you to answer me still.

What's the moral to the story?
She dies in the dream,
She waits for me to find love,
And following me-
Was her ego.
She spoke and I lived too close,
Lost my footsteps,
As she covered my throat.

Still searching for love,
I had search without,
Fantasies,
God cleared the wondrous clouds,
Wandering in a Magic Land,
I wondered myself,
And finally,

God revealed to me,
How it truly feels.
To feel love.

Through him; inside of me.

For The Lovers Pt.2

I never knew that love could take a person this far,
This high up – this low down,
I just know I've been to too many places trying to find it.

I found my inspiration to write this book when the wise ones had told
me,
"You don't know what love is."

Quite frankly, I don't, but on the other side of that, I do.
I know something.
I've felt something.
I dreamt and walked my days with something on my mind,
Pushing me to be better, to give more love, and expect less.

Some days, I would write these poems,
Only thinking of you,
And knowing that one day, you will read my stories not only to be
touched and taught,
But to understand and create your own vison of what love means to
you.

Like I said before, I am no expert on love.
I don't know all of the answers, but I know some.
I surely did not talk about everything that involves love,
I'm sure that I missed tons of ideas and scenarios,
I'm sure that some people may not fully understand each story, or
each of my vivid thoughts.
And what's special about that is, you don't have to.

This book, isn't only my book.
It is yours also,
As you read, you expanded your mind to follow my words,
I just illustrated what it looked like to me,
You saw it how you wanted to, remember?

To my lovers,
Look, learn, and listen.
We shall grow as one family.

We are the roses of our garden.

Teach the young, what it means to love.
You're never too young,
To teach the sprung,
How to spree.
Learn it. Live it. Give it
For one day, it will all come back to you.
I promise young love.

One love.

BENEDICTION

TO MY ROCK: *I love my mother with all of my heart. Never think that I don't see all of the things she does for me. My mother is the strongest woman I know. I would've never had the strength or mindset to write this book had it not been for her. I love you mom.*

TO BRADLEY BATTLES: *Teaching me the importance of humbleness and faithfulness unto God, and magnifying my blessings sent from God are the two most cherishing lessons I have received from you. Thank you for everything you have done for me, as well as my family. I appreciate you.*

AND TO MY FRIENDS: *I know you think you all know me – but y'all don't know me. I'm not as simple as I stand. I'm not just a funny kid who can write poems. I'm actually just like everyone. The funny thing is I swear I'm not like everyone. Sometimes in life people reach stages where there are only certain things that can help them. I feel that my writing and my prayers are my greatest remedies. I wish you guys really knew my pain, my stories, and my thoughts. I do this for you guys. I write this for you all. I love you all.*

TO MY BROTHER (JC): *I miss you dearly. I can never grasp the fact that you're not physically here with me. You were my best friend. If anyone, you understood me. You protected me and cared for me like no other. I dedicate this book to you. I hope heaven is sweeter than ice cream. Love you bro.*

TO THE LOVERS: *Love is not always something you go and find. You have to find yourself first. I know, everyone says that, but it's true. Take some time to find yourself, before you try to find love through others. Give love. Spread love. Receive love. Then, give some more. It's all about love. One love.*

TO THE R5WD (FAM): *Keep the cycle going. You guys inspired me to do this by showing me what love is. Reach one. Teach one. Breed one. Love.*

About The Author

Terrance Carter is a young poet who writes for other teens in an effort to assist them with understanding life experiences and making positive decisions for themselves.

This is Terrance's second published work of poems and prose. He recently graduated from Helix Charter High School in La Mesa, California and will be attending Grand Canyon University in the fall of 2015.

Out of all of the talents God has blessed me with, I chose to be an author because there is no greater feeling to me than influencing the millennial, my peers, family, and elders, through an artistic flow of my perspective. Many people have shared with me how much my writings have impacted them; as a young teenager, who has been through plenty, being a light unto the world is all that I have space to do. Every day I ask God to give me the strength to live out my purpose. Since I began writing, I have been reminded that this is my true gift. Thank you!